M000169431

Advance Praise

"Do you want to feel more confident about how to retire with more than enough income and still leave a legacy? With interesting and relevant stories from real families, Ryan and Tyson Thacker share their process—The B.O.S.S. Retirement Blueprint—to help make the most of your retirement so that you can minimize your stress (and taxes!) and maximize your enjoyment of this next phase of your life."
—Dan Sullivan, Founder of Strategic Coach®

"'The Retirement Brothers' take what's complex and make it simple and easy to understand. Ryan and Tyson have done it again with their latest book! They have a unique way of using the power of story to make financial

planning interesting and easy to understand. This is a must-read for anyone over fifty!"
—Joe Bayliss, published author, entrepreneur

"Tyson and Ryan have my complete trust and confidence. In a world full of doubt, polarization, and false messaging, Tyson and Ryan Thacker are unique professionals; they are the personification of ethical behavior and integrity with unparalleled professional acumen."
—Richard Doutre Jones,
VP/general manager Nexstar Broadcasting Inc.
(ABC4Utah, Utah's CW30, MeTV Utah)

"Having worked with Tyson and Ryan, it was evident from the first conversation how much these guys, and their entire team, care. Every interaction I've had with them is 100% about learning, growing, and serving, and for that reason, I am excited for this book to be in the hands of anyone aspiring to do more with what they have!"
—Ron Alford, senior partner,
Southwestern Consulting

"As I've come to know Tyson and Ryan, I've been impressed with the depth of their knowledge and their empathy towards others. Their approach to this industry is worthy of emulation."
—David McKnight, author of *The Power of Zero*

"In an industry where trust is hard-earned, Ryan and Tyson have gained it by doing things the right way."

—Gina Rainey, Advisors Excel

"As a fellow financial advisor and business owner, I have gotten to know both Ryan and Tyson pretty well over the past several years. They are both tremendous leaders and men, and their company takes the time and energy to help fulfill their passion of building their clients' true 'goals-based plans,' which we don't always see in the investment planning arena. I respect Tyson and Ryan not just as business leaders, but as excellent fathers, husbands, and friends."

—Derek L. Gregoire, founding partner,
SHP Financial

"I've known Ryan and Tyson for many years now. They are highly respected leaders in the financial industry and more importantly, they are men of impeccable integrity combined with practical experience and sound advice."

—C. Pete Benson,
senior partner, author, advisor

"I admire Ryan and Tyson for their passion of working with families to understand their financial goals and help build plans to achieve them. Their key differentiator is they do not consider themselves money managers, insurance people, or tax specialists, but problem solvers that leverage all financial tools to provide the most effective and tax efficient way for people to enjoy the best chapter in their lives! I wish more advisors thought this way!"

—Jim Bowman, Advisors Excel

"As I've worked with Tyson and Ryan, I've been impressed with how freely they share with all who could benefit from their knowledge and wisdom. Their generosity with all they come in contact with is a driving force behind the growth and success of their business."

—Cody Foster, Advisors Excel

"I've had the pleasure of getting to know Tyson and Ryan over the past several years. They are unquestioned leaders in the field of helping families plan for a secure retirement. You are about to enjoy a fantastic book where they share much of their knowledge. A great read—and great information."

—Michael D Reese, CFP, CEO,
Centennial Advisors

"The B.O.S.S. Retirement Blueprint will provide you wise counsel. This book is a cornerstone to help you prepare for a happy and carefree retirement."

—David Callanan, co-founder Advisors Excel

"The B.O.S.S. Retirement Blueprint is a wise, practical guide that simplifies the complex issues and questions of retirement into an intelligent, executable plan. I'm excited for you to have the benefit of their experience and expertise, to help fulfill your retirement dreams."

—Shannon Waller, entrepreneurial team strategist at The Strategic Coach

THE

B.O.S.S.

RETIREMENT
BLUEPRINT

YOUR GUIDE TO A SECURE
AND INDEPENDENT RETIREMENT

Tyson Thacker | Ryan Thacker

THE B.O.S.S. RETIREMENT BLUEPRINT
Your Guide to a Secure and Independent Retirement

ISBN 978-1-5445-0904-4 *Hardcover*
      978-1-5445-0902-0 *Paperback*
      978-1-5445-0903-7 *Ebook*

Contents

Introduction

Bob and Carol had both worked hard all their lives, saving and investing for their retirement. As this milestone drew nearer, though, they wondered if they'd done enough. Looking back over the years, they saw the patchwork of financial decisions they'd made. How did they fit together? What did those decisions mean to them now? What did they mean to their future? To their family's future?

Both Bob and Carol had a lot of concerns as they got closer to retirement. They were concerned about paying too much in taxes, the rising costs of healthcare, and— the big concern most people face in retirement—flat-out running out of money.

Their concerns were more than financial, though. They wanted to build their best life, not just their wealth, in their golden years. They both wanted to become more involved in service to their church and their community. They also wanted to pursue what they loved; Bob wanted the time and the means to hunt and fish more, and Carol wanted to further explore her passion for painting.

And then, the big one: family. The couple wanted to take trips with their kids and grandkids. They wanted to make memories. Like we all do, right?

But could they? Despite all their efforts to work hard and save over decades, was it even possible?

Their questions were valid and all-too-common. Did you know that 40% of Americans are at risk of going broke during their retirement years?[1] Did you know that whether you've saved a little or saved a lot, that percentage could still very well include you?

In this book, we'll get to know Bob and Carol well—their finances, their goals, and their outcome after working with our team of retirement advisors.

---

1 Angela Moore, "More Than 40% of Americans Are at Risk of Going Broke in Retirement—and That's the Good News," *MarketWatch,* May 12, 2018, https://www.marketwatch.com/story/now-the-bad-news-and-slightly-less-horrible-news-about-saving-for-retirement-2018-03-07.

In the meantime, let's answer the biggest question on your mind: what does this all mean to you?

MEMORIAL DAY MUDSLIDE...RETIREMENT REALITY

There are days in your life that you don't forget. A record snowfall in the winter of 1982 in the mountains of Utah led to floods and mudslides in 1983. On Memorial Day 1983, we were standing as a family watching our neighbor's cabin being pushed off its foundation by the mudslide. It completely destroyed their mountain dream.

What we didn't realize at the time was that the mudslide would expand. A crack came down through our cabin and cracked the foundation, threatening our mountain dream too. The Memorial Day mudslide of 1983 reminds us of the retirement crisis facing the majority of Americans today.

You're watching your neighbor's retirement get swept away by a mudslide of obstacles facing them, like no income plan, wild swings in the stock market, and taxes.

At first glance, you may think these issues will only affect your neighbor. Yet deep down inside you have a nagging feeling that bothers you every time you think about retirement. You may have realized that you don't know the answers to these same questions, and that is why you have picked up this book.

This is your wake-up call. Take a good look at where you could be and the obstacles that could be pushing your retirement off its foundation.

Many people believe only the poor lose everything in retirement, but in our experience helping thousands of families plan the financial foundation for their retirement years, that's not the case. Research shows that only half of Americans have more than $10,000 saved for retirement[2]—a statistic that doesn't much serve those sixty-five and older, as their average annual expenditure is almost four times that basic level of savings. If you have more in the bank, you're not out of the woods—not by a long shot.

The same considerations ring true regardless: you'll need to contend with issues surrounding income, risk, and taxes. Need proof? Look at the Vanderbilt family, who went from rags to riches to rags again. Besides a shipping empire, the family also had a monopoly within the railroad industry

---

2   Emmie Martin, "65% of Americans Save Little to Nothing—and Half Could End Up Struggling in Retirement," *CNBC*, March 15, 2018, https://www.cnbc.com/2018/03/15/bankrate-65-percent-of-americans-save-little-or-nothing.html.

after the Civil War, specifically over trains going in and out of New York. The patriarch who built the fortune, Cornelius Vanderbilt, left his wealth to his two sons, one of whom— William—is credited with doubling the already immense fortune. Then, when William passed in 1899 and left that wealth to his sons, they (and their spouses) squandered it (namely William, his father's namesake), spending money on lavish parties, mansions, real estate, and the like. In the 1920s, the excess took its toll, and a majority of the wealth was lost for good.[3] This notable family case is no family secret: even the wealthy can go broke in retirement, and that's not what we want for you. You need to have a plan—a financial blueprint for retirement results!

Imagine walking out of your last day of work, looking forward to what retirement will bring. You're excited to spend more time with your family. Excited to travel. Excited to relax. Excited to make a new set of memories. And then you get a wake-up call to the complicated and confusing obstacles of navigating retirement. We don't want that to happen to you!

On average, Social Security will cover only about one-third of your income. If you were planning on Social Security covering your expenses, you may be in for a

---

3 "Riches to Rags: The Fall of the Celebrated Vanderbilt Family," *History Things*, December 6, 2016, https://historythings.com/riches-rags-fall-cele-brated-vanderbilt-family/.

shock. What happens if you have to dip into your savings more often than you'd like? What happens if you face skyrocketing medical expenses? After all, most retiring couples are shocked that they will pay out of pocket an average of almost $390,000 in medical expenses during their retirement years.[4] What happens if the market takes a 30%, 40%, or 50% dip—or more, as it sometimes does—and you lose a significant portion of your retirement savings? What happens when you try to pull out some of your money, and Uncle Sam takes a third or more of it in taxes?

In reality, retirement is just like being unemployed for twenty or thirty more years: seeing how much you have in the bank, how much your monthly check is, and what your expenses are. In one quick calculation, you can figure out how long you'll be able to stay afloat if you don't go back to work. If you're in the situation where you have to make that calculation, though, you're already starting to sink.

We know that's not the retirement you dreamed of when you triumphantly walked out of work that last time. Still, the facts remain: at the end of the day, 60% of Americans retire before they think they want to, and most won't retire

---

4   Darla Mercado, "Retiring This Year? How Much You'll Need For Health-Care Costs," *CNBC*, July 18, 2019, https://www.cnbc.com/2019/07/18/retiring-this-year-how-much-youll-need-for-health-care-costs.html.

on their own terms.[5] We don't want that to be you—and we have a plan that can help.

But first, let us introduce ourselves.

SUNDAY SUPPER AROUND THE DINNER TABLE

You only retire once, and our mission is to help you do it right. We are Tyson and Ryan Thacker, the founders of B.O.S.S. Retirement Solutions and Advisors. As the fifth and sixth born into a family of seven kids, we've shared decades of Sunday afternoon meals together.

Those meals looked like this: picture a perfect spring day. You walk in the door, and you can smell the roast beef cooking and see the mashed potatoes on the table. Your mouth is watering. The environment is so welcoming, setting the place where we all feel comfortable talking about both our successes and setbacks together. It's a place of refuge, a safe space, a supportive space. It's also a place with the best yellow cake and homemade chocolate frosting.

---

5   Charisse Jones, "60% of Americans Have to Retire Sooner Than They'd Planned," *USA Today*, June 3, 2015, https://www.usatoday.com/story/money/2015/06/02/majority-of-americans-have-to-retire-sooner-than-theyd-planned/28371099/.

Sitting together as a family, we talked about what matters most.

We *still* talk about what matters most, and we've built our careers as "The Retirement Brothers." We are dedicated to helping you build a secure retirement. We are grateful we have been recognized as Utah's Best of State for Retirement Planning for 3 years in a row. We've also been recognized nationally on the Inc. 5000 list of America's fastest growing companies for the last five consecutive years!

But what we are most proud of is that through our books, radio show, and television show, we've helped thousands of families like yours build a plan to walk away with more of what they've earned, grow it, and use it to leave a legacy they're proud of.

This isn't simply our job. This is our mission.

We believe in simplicity, in taking complex financial problems and making them make sense. In this book, we'll discuss the key principles of our B.O.S.S. Retirement Blueprint™—a simple, one-page document we help you create that you can use to get to and through retirement with ease. Along the way, we'll share our own stories—experiences we had growing up in the mountains of Utah that contributed to our approach today, how we've leaned on our families along the way, and what leaving a legacy truly means to us.

This is *not* a do-it-yourself retirement or financial planning book. It *is* a book that helps explain the obstacles associated with retirement, the value of having a plan, and the importance of having help to guide you along your journey. Think of us like your brothers who can guide you to and through retirement.

In reading this book, you're joining us at our family table. Welcome!

Part I

America's Retirement Crisis

1

The Income Problem

The problem for most Americans is that they haven't thought about where their income will come from in retirement. That is like a farmer who has no idea where their water will come from and hoping it will rain enough to water their crops…not a good idea.

Have you ever thought about retirement and asked yourself, "Do I have enough money, and am I going to run out?" That's the number one question families ask us in our office conference rooms, and for good reason. It's human nature to want to feel secure.

We've already mentioned that just under half of all Americans are at risk of going broke during retirement, so the question is more than valid. In real estate, the three magic words are "location, location, location."

In retirement, the three magic words are "income, income, income." The problem? Generating income in retirement grows more complicated by the day.

Our dad grew up on a farm in the Heber Valley in the shadow of Mount Timpanogos in the majestic Wasatch mountains. The farm had a stream that came from Daniels Canyon, which was fed by springs filled by snowcapped mountains.

On Dad's farm, there was a spring that flowed year-round. Dad taught us that this was a water source that needed to be protected. It had a fence around it to keep the cows out of the spring, and on hot summer days, we loved to get a drink from that spring. Dad taught us that the water came directly from the base of the mountain and it was pure, so we could drink it and not worry about getting sick.

As kids, Dad taught us that you protect your water. He taught us to make sure you know where your water is coming from to irrigate your fields because the quality and quantity of crops in your fields equal the amount of money that you will live on in your retirement years. Land without water, especially in the high mountain desert of Utah, is worthless. Just like a retirement without income is worthless and downright dangerous.

In retirement, you need to know where your water comes from. Your life-sustaining water in retirement is income. We recommend you have at least three resources of income as part of your plan in retirement.

Most of you reading this will have Social Security as one source, and if you are part of the lucky 18% of Americans who have a pension, you might have two. That means you're likely still missing at least one more source of income for your retirement years.

Why? In the old days, you worked at the same company for thirty years—your entire career, mostly—and then you reached age sixty-five. They had a party for you, and maybe you even got a gold watch. Then, you got a paycheck for the rest of your life called a pension.

Sounds great, right? Retirement expert Tom Hegna wrote about this in his book *Paychecks and Playchecks: Retirement Solutions for Life*. Today, only 18% of Americans have a pension. At the end of 2017, the Pension Benefit Guaranty Corporation (PBGC)—which is to pensions as the Federal Deposit Insurance Corporation (FDIC) is to banks—was $76 billion in debt—and things are not exactly looking up. The head of the PBGC has warned Congress that those 18% of people who still have a pension could see their benefits cut by as much as a whopping 90%.[6]

Faltering pensions aren't the only problem. Numbers-wise, more than 80% of you don't have a pension, anyway, and we've just learned that those who do may see mere pennies on the dollar. Still, there are far more issues to contend with in the income bucket: namely, Social Security and inflation. Social Security is not on the same stable foundation that everyone once thought it was—it's just another busted "paycheck for the rest of your life" dream that's potentially not going to come true, or at least come true enough to sustain you. In addition, we're living longer than we ever have—there are approximately 450,000 people living today who are over the age of one hundred. In the next thirty years, that figure will balloon to 3.7 million.[7]

---

6   Jordan Wathen, "Pensions Are Disappearing, Here's How to Save for Retirement," *The Motley Fool*, June 5, 2018, https://www.fool.com/investing/2018/06/05/pensions-are-disappearing-heres-how-to-save-for-re.aspx.

7   Renee Stepler, "World's Centenarian Population Projected to Grow Eightfold by 2050," *Pew Research Center,* April 21, 2016, https://www.pewresearch.org/fact-tank/2016/04/21/worlds-centenarian-population-projected-to-grow-eightfold-by-2050/.

As a columnist for *Kiplinger* reported,[8] asking the question about how far one dollar gets you in retirement "is the same as getting into your car for a trip from Boston to Washington, DC. Rather than checking the mileage or traffic, you tell your passengers that we'll go as far as the gas in the tank will take us. You also know that, depending on conditions, you might run dry in Baltimore."

The trick is to plan for income, not savings—and even then, that income should be reliable so that it doesn't depend on the performance of something you can't control, like the stock market.

When you retire, life and its expenses don't stop happening. That's why the only thing close to a "magic" number should be how much income you need to cover your lifestyle. Then, you can calculate what income you need—and where it is coming from.

Are you a single mom who has pulled yourself up by your bootstraps to help your family survive? Maybe you've figured you only need $2,500 a month for retirement because you've paid off your home.

---

8 Jerry Golden, "The Million-Dollar Retirement Question Is All Wrong," *Kiplinger,* May 15, 2018, https://www.kiplinger.com/article/retirement/T047-C032-S014-the-million-dollar-retirement-question-is-wrong.html.

Are you a company executive who currently spends $25,000 a month and wants to be able to continue that lifestyle in retirement?

The circumstances are different, but the question is the same: will your income last as long as your retirement does?

If you're relying on Social Security alone, that answer is likely no. Let's talk about the elephant in the room.

THE PROBLEM WITH SOCIAL SECURITY

If you take your Social Security at face value—in other words, you look at your statement and pick an age (like sixty-two or sixty-seven)—you could make a mistake that could cost you tens of thousands, if not hundreds of thousands, of dollars in retirement.

Why? Claiming your Social Security benefits could trigger an avalanche of taxes, double your Medicare premiums, and cause you to leave benefits on the table. In fact, according to *Forbes Magazine*, as much as $10 billion in Social Security benefits go unclaimed every year.

If you don't have a plan for how and when you're going to take your benefits, odds are that you'll be one of them.

Another issue is that creating that plan is confusing in and of itself unless you work with an expert. There are 2,728 rules in the Social Security handbook, and thousands of rules that branch from those rules. Too many people ask a friend or a neighbor when they took Social Security, fill out a form online, and call it done. They have no idea they may be taxed on as much as 85% of their benefits. They have no idea they have other options or that there are more ways to squeeze income from their benefit plans.

Lawrence Kotlikoff, Professor of Economics at Boston University and an expert on Social Security, did an audit of when people visit the Social Security website. He found an excess of vague language—perhaps an attempt by the government to streamline information, but an attempt that resulted in site visitors without a guide feeling confused and no more informed than before. This is not right, as a married couple will likely put north of six figures into their Social Security over their adult lives—money that is theirs. One wrong move, though, and they'd get a vastly different result.

The most common questions we get asked about Social Security are strikingly basic. We love helping our clients answer these questions, but they also show how much simple knowledge is missing out there among those not working with guides:

- At what age should I take my Social Security?

- How do I avoid making costly mistakes
  when it comes to my Social Security?

- What happens to my Social Security when I
  die? Can I pass it to my partner and kids?

- Are there any strategies to maximizing and opti-
  mizing my Social Security? Is that even possible?

This is just the tip of the Social Security iceberg. After all, according to new research featured in *Bloomberg*...96% of hardworking Americans lose an average of $111,000 in Social Security benefits. And it's all due to critical timing mistakes.[9] The bottom line is simple: you only retire once with Social Security, and you've got do to it right. There are no do-overs.

You only retire once. Doing it right matters.

GETTING MUGGED BY INFLATION

---

9   Ben Steverman, "Americans Lose Trillions Claiming Social Security at the Wrong Time," *Bloomberg,* June 27, 2019, https://www.bloomberg.com/news/articles/2019-06-28/americans-lose-trillions-claiming-social-security-at-the-wrong-time.

Ronald Reagan once said, "Inflation is as violent as a mugger."

He was right. He witnessed how double-digit inflation in the late seventies and eighties could have a devastating impact on your money. You probably remember these days as well...and likely had a double-digit mortgage rate on your home because of inflation!

Inflation is why you continue to lose the value of a dollar — in fact, just in the last decade, it has stripped 21% of the value of a dollar.

It's easier to understand inflation when we describe it using common items. For example, $1.00 in 1950 is equal to $10.65 in 2019.[10] In 1930, the average cost of a pound of hamburger meat was $0.12; in 2017, it was $4.68.[11] Increases of 1%, 2%, or even 3% may not seem like much, but if you add it up over twenty or thirty years, it could have a huge impact on your lifestyle in retirement. That's why they call inflation the "silent killer."

---

10   "Calculate the Value of $1.00 in 1950: What is $1 in 1950 Worth in To-day's Money?" *DollarTimes*, https://www.dollartimes.com/inflation/inflation.php?amount=1&year=1950.

11   "Comparison of Prices over 90 Years," *The People History*, http://www.thepeoplehistory.com/70yearsofpricechange.html.

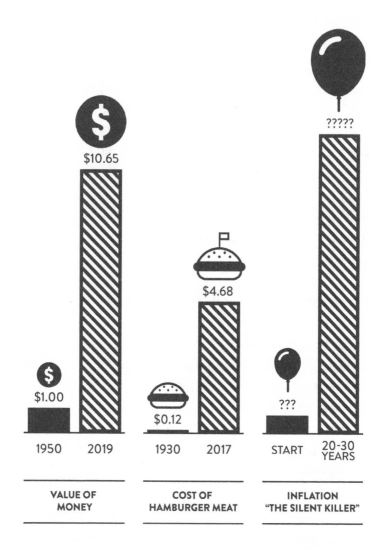

| VALUE OF MONEY | COST OF HAMBURGER MEAT | INFLATION "THE SILENT KILLER" |

The more inflation increases, the more the cost of everything increases—especially healthcare, which already increases at a rate higher than inflation. (This is not great news for the retirement community.) For example, "Employer healthcare costs in the US are rising 6.5% in 2020 or nearly double the rate of general inflation for yet another year…"[12]

It's possible you remember the effect of inflation back in the late seventies and early eighties. We sure do. As a family, people in our neighborhood were losing their homes as interest rates skyrocketed and people lost their jobs. It makes us emotional to think about what could happen if you don't understand and plan for inflation: you could literally end up being eighty-five years old, full of life, and flat broke.

Numbers-wise, if you're sixty-two years old right now and spending $5,000 a month, by the time you're eighty-two, you'll need nearly $10,000 a month to meet those same basic needs—and that's just with the inflation rate as-is, over the last hundred years.

---

12   Bruce Japsen, "In 2020, Employer Health Costs to Double Inflation Yet Again," *Forbes,* September 12, 2019, https://www.forbes.com/sites/brucejapsen/2019/09/12/in-2020-employer-health-costs-to-double-inflation-rate-yet-again/?sh=128432d22754.

Put simply, this means ignoring inflation could mean the difference between you enjoying everything you've ever dreamed of doing in retirement versus just getting by.

CASE STUDY:
BOB AND CAROL'S INCOME PROBLEM

Bob and Carol recognize Social Security is an important source of retirement income, but they don't have another plan. They're confused and don't understand how to maximize or optimize their Social Security income. They have also heard they could be taxed on their Social Security benefits, and they don't want to make a mistake that could cost them tens of thousands—if not hundreds of thousands—of dollars during retirement.

WHAT I WANT

RETIREMENT INCOME

TARGET INCOME	$ 5,830
SOCIAL SECURITY	$ 2,975
SOCIAL SECURITY	$ 1,968
PENSION	$
OTHER	$
OTHER	$
TOTAL INCOME	$ 4,943
SHORTFALL/ SURPLUS	$ -887

They also have an income shortfall in retirement. Their income goal is $5,000 per month—which, with inflation, is more like $5,830. Bob's Social Security is $2,975 and Carol's is $1,968, for a total of $4,943. That investment leaves them with an $887 shortfall, after we factor in inflation.

WHAT'S NEXT?

Let's go back, for a moment, to farmers knowing where their water comes from. In life, you need to know where your income in retirement will come from.

If your retirement income plan depends solely on Social Security—especially if it doesn't account for inflation— you're in the same boat. You may run out of money before you run out of life, and no one wants to be eighty-five years old…full of life…and flat broke!

If you think you can hit a "magic number" by how much you have saved for retirement and that your retirement is golden, you're setting yourself up for disaster. What if one income source dries up and you don't have a well-diversified retirement income plan? It could be a disaster, just like the Memorial Day mudslide of 1983.

Too many people wind up scraping by in retirement—even those who started with money. In Part II, we'll show you how to avoid this nightmare. First, though, let's discuss the risks and myths associated with growing and protecting what you have worked so hard to save.

2

The Growth versus Risk Problem

Do you want a risky plan to potentially be rich in retirement? Or do you want a plan to not be poor in retirement?

We have asked this question over and over to the thousands of families we serve, and the overwhelming majority respond that they want a plan to not be poor in retirement.

Hindsight is always 20/20, and after the recent financial meltdowns in 2001, 2008, and now the COVID-19 crisis of 2020, Americans are seeking and demanding financial results. More than ever, Americans are questioning why they are doing what they are doing with their money.

Years ago, when we started searching for the most reliable way to safely grow money for retirement, we started searching for answers to financial questions. We started to challenge the status quo and question why we were doing what we were doing. We later learned that what we were doing was what our mentor and coach Dan Sullivan would call "thinking about your thinking."[13]

After college we worked for a company in the mortgage banking industry that offered a benefits package with a respectable match of 6% to our 401(k) contributions. Our careers were taking off and we were reaching and exceeding every goal that we had set when we graduated from college. We were doing our best to follow all of the traditional financial advice we had learned in college.

We wanted to plan for our future. In addition, we saw how pensions were changing and knew that a few companies had already defaulted on the promises they had made to their dedicated and loyal employees.

---

13   Dan Sullivan, "The Transformative Power of Thinking about Your Thinking," *Strategic Coach*, https://resources.strategiccoach.com/the-multiplier-mindset-blog/the-transformative-power-of-thinking-about-your-thinking-2.

We were committed to contributing the maximum allowed to our own retirement using a 401(k) or qualified retirement plan. Although it was difficult, we did our best to follow the familiar path, which included:

- Save three to six months of living expenses in an emergency fund.

- Pay off all consumer debt (cars, credit cards, etc.).

- Max out your 401(k), IRA, or qualified retirement account.

- Buy term life insurance and "invest" the difference.

- Dollar cost average into the stock market using index funds or mutual funds.

- Pay down your mortgage as fast as possible.

In addition to these goals, we started investing heavily in real estate and applying the knowledge we had learned from our banking background. We continued to read and learn everything we could about real estate and investing. This came to us very easily because of our background in business and banking. We had many contacts with Realtors, title companies, and appraisers. These

contacts often provided us many opportunities to partic-
ipate in our own real estate projects.

LOSING CONTROL

Eventually we reached a crossroads where our perfect financial plan—including contributions to our 401(k) accounts,
accelerated mortgage payments, and mutual funds—had
a head-on collision with our real estate investing.

Each time we put money into our 401(k) accounts, that
money was locked away until we reached age fifty-nine
and a half, and heavy restrictions affected our ability to
access funds from the accounts. If we pulled the money
out for more than sixty days, we would be taxed on the
entire amount and face a stiff 10% penalty.

In addition, we realized that if we paid additional payments
down on our mortgages, that money was no longer
liquid. In other words, the only way to access our equity
was to sell the homes or take out new loans to access
the money that we had paid the mortgage company.

Finally, our monthly investment into mutual funds seemed
more and more like a losing proposition. It seemed like the
only time our account balances moved in a positive direc-

tion was when we deposited our monthly investments into the accounts. We felt like we were losing control of our money each time we followed conventional wisdom by paying into our 401(k)s, paying down our mortgages, or investing in the stock market. We were forced to slow our progress of making investments in real estate because we no longer had additional funds to use for down payments on properties. This was extremely frustrating, considering we knew and understood our local real estate market as well as most experts in the area.

CRACK IN THE FOUNDATION?

As we look back, we realize that this challenge was a blessing in our lives. We started to see that our traditional financial plan had some serious cracks in its foundation. We started to ask tough questions of our advisors—and to do some relatively simple math.

We asked questions such as: "Is this 401(k) really a great deal?

"We like the pre-tax contributions and the tax-deferred growth, but does that make long-term sense if I am possibly going to be taxed at a higher rate when I withdraw the funds at retirement?

"If taxes are most likely going to increase in the future, why do we want to postpone the payment of taxes when we are likely to be paying higher, not lower, taxes?"

We liked the Roth IRA concept, but we didn't like the income restrictions and contribution limits that prevented us from contributing more to a Roth IRA.

We also started to question why we were doing what we were doing! Why were we taking all the risk when we invested our hard-earned money when we had learned banks take very little risk with their money?

As we began to look for answers to our questions, we discovered some financial myths and cracks in the foundation of the traditional plan we were following, which likely is the same plan most of you have followed to this point in your lives.

While we could look at many different topics, we feel there are three myths that continue to be perpetuated by the media and financial gurus. The three myths we will address in this chapter are:

1. You can save your way to a magic retirement number.

2. Calculating an average rate of return doesn't always translate into the growth of money that shows up in your retirement account.

3. High risk equates to a high reward.

MYTH NUMBER ONE: YOU CAN SAVE YOUR WAY TO A MAGIC RETIREMENT NUMBER

Most Americans have lost sight of why they are saving and investing. A dangerous myth is that we can save our way to a magic retirement number. The reason this myth is so dangerous is because you don't live off an account balance…your retirement success is about generating reliable retirement income.

Think about your financial goals and objectives for a moment. Why are you saving and investing? What are you saving and investing for?

Most of you are simply on autopilot, hoping that if you set aside a percentage of your income into a 401(k), IRA, or some other retirement vehicle, magically you will have a large balance in your account when it comes time to retire.

Most of you recognize that you need to set money aside for the future. In fact, you have been bombarded with the financial message that we need to save and invest for retirement.

However, you don't spend account balances in retirement...you spend income!

If money is not distributed properly, you could run out of money before you run out of life!

Hoping you have enough money for the future is not a financial strategy. Let this serve as your wake-up call! The reality is that whatever vehicle you are using to build and accumulate wealth will at some point need to create a reliable retirement income that will allow you to pay your expenses and pay for all the things you have dreamed of, like traveling, playing golf, visiting grandkids, or donating your time to your favorite charity when you retire.

Statistically speaking, fewer than 10% of you will be able to do the things you chose because you are trying to save your way to a magic number, and you do not have a retirement income plan. The good news is that there are financial strategies to help you turn your hard-earned savings into an income workhorse to get you to and through retirement.

Consider the example of two retired couples who are the same age (sixty-seven). They have saved the same amount of money ($1 million), yet they are living two completely different lifestyles in retirement. One of them is living it up, while the other...is just scared of where their income is going to come from each month and does not have an income plan.

How does this happen and why? The difference between these two couples is that one has a strategy and plan to generate consistent income, and the other doesn't. We've seen this too many times, and we want you to avoid the stress and anxiety couple number two felt throughout their retirement.

Couple one has worked with a professional to create a full plan that includes three sources of consistent income. The first income source is the foundation to all income: Social Security. Couple number one has Social Security of $1,750 for the husband and $2,250 for the wife, for a total of $4,000 per month. The second income stream is an income annuity paying $1,750 per month in income. Lastly, they have some money from a conservative bond portfolio and some dividend-paying stocks averaging $500 per month. The total income is a reliable $6,250 per month or $75,000 per year.

COUPLE ONE: MONTHLY INCOME

SOCIAL SECURITY

1 HUSBAND $1,750
       + WIFE $2,250
       _____
       S.S. TOTAL **$4,000**

2 + INCOME
          ANNUITY **$1,750**

3 + STOCKS &
          BONDS **$500**

_____

MONTHLY INCOME **$6,250**
x12 = ANNUAL INCOME $75,000

HAPPY COUPLE
BECAUSE NO CHANGE
IN INCOME AFTER
STOCK MARKET DROP!

Couple number two has been earning more than 7.5% on average over the last ten years in their retirement accounts and feels confident that they can continue down that path throughout retirement. They figure if they can generate the same 7.5% in the future, they will rely on growth for their income plan and that they should have more than enough to live off for the rest of their lives, especially once they start taking Social Security.

Here's where couple number two's strategy goes off the rails. Within the first months of retirement, the stock market drops 42%. This means their retirement nest egg drops to $580,000, leaving them in a dilemma that we call in the industry "sequence of returns risk." Now the couple's need for $75,000 per year does not look very reliable and requires a 12.9% withdrawal from the couple's investments, which could mean they will run out of money before they run out of life!

To be blunt, sequence of returns risk is a threat they never saw coming. This is the risk of retiring in a bear market. Couple number two still has to withdraw money to live on, and in their case they must either live off much less or eat deeply into their principal. If, like this couple, you must withdraw money while the market is down, you could be in big trouble.

The returns you compound during your first five to ten years of retirement are critical to your success. Retiring in a bear market could have significant consequences on your savings and investments. Those who retire in a bull market fare significantly better than those who don't.

COUPLE TWO: MONTHLY INCOME

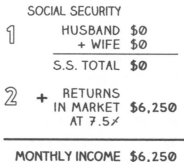

```
        SOCIAL SECURITY
 1         HUSBAND  $0
           + WIFE   $0
           ─────────────
          S.S. TOTAL  $0

 2    +   RETURNS
          IN MARKET  $6,250
          AT 7.5⊁
      ─────────────────────
      MONTHLY INCOME  $6,250
      x12 = ANNUAL INCOME $75,000
```

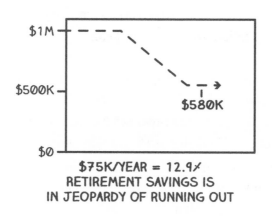

$75K/YEAR = 12.9⊁
RETIREMENT SAVINGS IS
IN JEOPARDY OF RUNNING OUT

Even if short-term volatility averages out into strong long-term returns, retirees could still be in hot water if the sequence of those returns is bad at the very beginning of retirement.

Required minimum distributions (RMDs) could pose a major threat during bear markets. You will be forced to sell your investments in your retirement accounts when markets are down, whether you want to or not.

Can you see why it's so important to plan instead of using general rules of thumb?

Income Goal of $75,000 per Year	Income Goal of $75,000 per Year
1. Social Security: $4,000/month	**1.** Social Security: $0/month
2. Income Annuity: $1,750/month	**2.** Returns in Market at 7.5%: $6,250
3. Bond/Dividends: $500/month	
4. Total Monthly Income = $6,250	After-Drop Balance $580,000-Income: $0

MYTH NUMBER TWO: AVERAGE RATE OF RETURN DOESN'T TRANSLATE INTO MONEY IN YOUR ACCOUNT

People look at their investment prospectus or past rates of return earned (or money previously lost), and that lulls them into a false sense of security. The investments they choose or the financial professionals they work with all carry charts showing impressive historical averages. You calculate your magic retirement number using this average rate of return and assume that past performance will equate to future returns. Unfortunately, most of the time this simply does not work.

As part of this thinking, we'd like to dismantle the myth of average rates of return. What is not well understood is that the returns in your pocket can be very different from the average rate of return you see in a mutual fund or index fund prospectus. Let's stay simple and look at a $100,000 investment over a four-year period.

To prove our point, let's use a hypothetical return of a mutual fund that claims to have had an average rate of return of 25%. The number really could be any number, but we want you to see that an average rate of return does not always mean your money has grown by 25% each year:

- Year 1: +100% growth

- Year 2: –50% loss

- Year 3: +100% growth

- Year 4: –50% loss

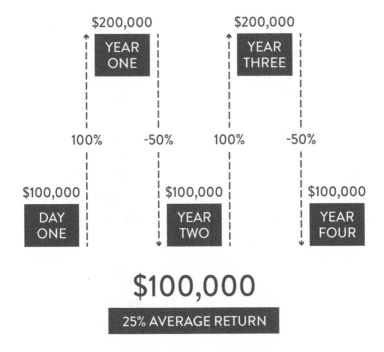

$100,000
25% AVERAGE RETURN

So, for four years you've had this money invested, and you have not made a dime. In fact, after fund fees, you probably have less than your initial investment. If you average 100% up, 50% down, 100% up, and 50% down, the average rate of return for those four years equals 25%.

We know some of you may be saying, "That is a ridiculous example of an average rate of return." Being ridiculous is exactly our point. Average rate of return is a ridiculous way to measure. Instead, it's best to measure the money that is actually in your retirement accounts generated from real growth instead of simply looking at average rates of return.

We understand that returns can be measured by average rate of return or geometric rate of return—however, the most important measurement is what is in your account at the end of the investment period. Average or geometric, the real result or spendable dollar amount in your account is what matters most!

If you lose 50% in the value of a mutual fund, you must have a 100% return in the fund to break even from your losses. It may take years to break even, let alone have any growth in the account.

In short, you need a plan that matches your appetite for risk and puts real money in your pocket during retirement.

MYTH NUMBER THREE: HIGH RISK EQUALS HIGH REWARD

People get hoodwinked all the time when it comes to the market—chasing high returns, not being sure how to protect against loss, not understanding who they should be listening to, etc.

One thing history teaches us is that just because an investment was hot last year, it doesn't mean it will perform well next year. As you know, "Past performance does not guarantee future results."

The mistake many investors make is chasing the investment that had the highest return last year. Usually by the time they invest in the high-performing stock or mutual fund, the growth trend is over. They see little growth, or maybe the trend even reverses.

The investment consulting firm Callan is famous for the Callan Periodic Table of Investment Returns. It is sometimes referred to as the "Skittles chart" of investment returns by asset class because of the varied colors they use in the chart. If you'd like to see the chart in color you can go to: https://www.callan.com/periodic-table/.

This chart makes the case for diversification instead of chasing the hottest yearly asset class.

In the chart below, you can see all the primary asset classes you had the opportunity to invest in from 2000 to 2019. If you search for the darkest box, you'll find the large-cap growth asset class.

If you draw a line and follow the ups and downs of the large-cap growth asset class, you'll see that if you'd

The Callan Periodic Table of Investment Returns
Annual Returns for Key Indices Ranked in Order of Performance (2001–2020)

2001	2002	2003	2004	2005	2006	2007	2008	2009	2010	2011	2012	2013	2014	2015	2016	2017	2018	2019	2020
U.S. Fixed Income 8.43%	Gbl ex-U.S. Fixed 22.37%	Emerging Market Equity 55.82%	Real Estate 37.96%	Emerging Market Equity 34.00%	Real Estate 42.12%	Emerging Market Equity 39.38%	U.S. Fixed Income 5.24%	Emerging Market Equity 79.51%	Small Cap Equity 26.85%	U.S. Fixed Income 7.84%	Real Estate 27.73%	Small Cap Equity 38.82%	Real Estate 15.02%	Large Cap Equity 1.38%	Small Cap Equity 21.31%	Emerging Market Equity 37.28%	Cash Equivalent 1.87%	Large Cap Equity 31.49%	Small Cap Equity 19.96%
High Yield 5.28%	U.S. Fixed Income 10.26%	Small Cap Equity 47.25%	Emerging Market Equity 25.55%	Real Estate 15.35%	Emerging Market Equity 32.17%	Dev ex-U.S. Equity 12.44%	Gbl ex-U.S. Fixed 4.39%	High Yield 58.21%	Real Estate 19.63%	High Yield 4.98%	Emerging Market Equity 18.23%	Large Cap Equity 32.39%	Large Cap Equity 13.69%	U.S. Fixed Income 0.55%	High Yield 17.13%	Dev ex-U.S. Equity 24.21%	U.S. Fixed Income 0.01%	Small Cap Equity 25.52%	Large Cap Equity 18.40%
Cash Equivalent 4.42%	Real Estate 2.82%	Real Estate 40.69%	Dev ex-U.S. Equity 20.38%	Dev ex-U.S. Equity 14.47%	Dev ex-U.S. Equity 25.71%	Gbl ex-U.S. Fixed 11.03%	Cash Equivalent 2.06%	Real Estate 37.13%	Emerging Market Equity 18.88%	Gbl ex-U.S. Fixed 4.36%	Dev ex-U.S. Equity 16.41%	Dev ex-U.S. Equity 21.02%	U.S. Fixed Income 5.97%	Cash Equivalent 0.05%	Large Cap Equity 11.96%	Large Cap Equity 21.83%	High Yield -2.08%	Dev ex-U.S. Equity 22.49%	Emerging Market Equity 18.31%
Small Cap Equity 2.49%	Cash Equivalent 1.78%	Dev ex-U.S. Equity 39.42%	Small Cap Equity 18.33%	Large Cap Equity 4.91%	Small Cap Equity 18.37%	U.S. Fixed Income 6.97%	High Yield -26.16%	Dev ex-U.S. Equity 33.67%	High Yield 15.12%	Large Cap Equity 2.11%	Small Cap Equity 16.35%	High Yield 7.44%	Small Cap Equity 4.89%	Real Estate -0.79%	Emerging Market Equity 11.19%	Small Cap Equity 14.65%	Gbl ex-U.S. Fixed -2.15%	Real Estate 21.91%	Gbl ex-U.S. Fixed 10.11%
Emerging Market Equity -2.61%	High Yield -1.37%	High Yield 28.97%	Gbl ex-U.S. Fixed 12.54%	Small Cap Equity 4.55%	Large Cap Equity 15.79%	Large Cap Equity 5.49%	Small Cap Equity -33.79%	Small Cap Equity 27.17%	Large Cap Equity 15.06%	Cash Equivalent 0.10%	Large Cap Equity 16.00%	Real Estate 3.67%	High Yield 2.45%	Dev ex-U.S. Equity -3.04%	Real Estate 4.06%	Gbl ex-U.S. Fixed 10.51%	Large Cap Equity -4.38%	Emerging Market Equity 18.44%	Dev ex-U.S. Equity 7.59%
Gbl ex-U.S. Fixed -3.75%	Emerging Market Equity -6.16%	Large Cap Equity 28.68%	High Yield 11.13%	Cash Equivalent 3.07%	High Yield 11.85%	Cash Equivalent 5.00%	Large Cap Equity -37.00%	Large Cap Equity 26.47%	Dev ex-U.S. Equity 8.95%	Small Cap Equity -4.18%	High Yield 15.81%	Cash Equivalent 0.07%	Cash Equivalent 0.03%	Small Cap Equity -4.41%	Dev ex-U.S. Equity 2.75%	Real Estate 10.36%	Real Estate -5.63%	High Yield 14.32%	U.S. Fixed Income 7.51%
Real Estate -3.81%	Dev ex-U.S. Equity -15.80%	Gbl ex-U.S. Fixed 18.36%	Large Cap Equity 10.88%	High Yield 2.74%	Gbl ex-U.S. Fixed 8.16%	High Yield 1.87%	Dev ex-U.S. Equity -43.56%	Gbl ex-U.S. Fixed 7.53%	U.S. Fixed Income 6.54%	Real Estate -6.46%	U.S. Fixed Income 4.21%	U.S. Fixed Income -2.02%	Emerging Market Equity -2.19%	High Yield -4.47%	U.S. Fixed Income 2.65%	High Yield 7.50%	Small Cap Equity -11.01%	U.S. Fixed Income 8.72%	High Yield 7.11%
Large Cap Equity -11.89%	Small Cap Equity -20.48%	U.S. Fixed Income 4.10%	U.S. Fixed Income 4.34%	U.S. Fixed Income 2.43%	Cash Equivalent 4.85%	Small Cap Equity -1.57%	Real Estate -48.21%	U.S. Fixed Income 5.93%	Gbl ex-U.S. Fixed 4.95%	Dev ex-U.S. Equity -12.21%	Gbl ex-U.S. Fixed 4.09%	Emerging Market Equity -2.60%	Gbl ex-U.S. Fixed -3.09%	Gbl ex-U.S. Fixed -6.02%	Gbl ex-U.S. Fixed 1.49%	U.S. Fixed Income 3.54%	Dev ex-U.S. Equity -14.09%	Gbl ex-U.S. Fixed 5.09%	Cash Equivalent 0.67%
Dev ex-U.S. Equity -21.40%	Large Cap Equity -22.10%	Cash Equivalent 1.15%	Cash Equivalent 1.33%	Gbl ex-U.S. Fixed -8.65%	U.S. Fixed Income 4.33%	Real Estate -7.39%	Emerging Market Equity -53.33%	Cash Equivalent 0.21%	Cash Equivalent 0.13%	Emerging Market Equity -18.42%	Cash Equivalent 0.11%	Gbl ex-U.S. Fixed -3.08%	Dev ex-U.S. Equity -4.32%	Emerging Market Equity -14.92%	Cash Equivalent 0.33%	Cash Equivalent 0.86%	Emerging Market Equity -14.57%	Cash Equivalent 2.28%	Real Estate -9.04%

The Callan Periodic Table of Investment Returns conveys the strong *case for diversification* across asset classes (stocks vs. bonds), capitalizations (large vs. small), and equity markets (U.S. vs. global ex-U.S.). The Table highlights the uncertainty inherent in all capital markets. Rankings change every year. Also noteworthy is the difference between absolute and relative performance, as returns for the top-performing asset class span a wide range over the past 20 years.

A printable copy of The Callan Periodic Table of Investment Returns is available on our website at callan.com.

The Callan Periodic Table of Investment Returns 2001–2020

Callan's Periodic Table of Investment Returns depicts annual returns for 8 asset classes and cash equivalents, ranked from best to worst performance for each calendar year. The asset classes are color-coded to enable easy tracking over time. We describe the well-known, industry-standard market indices that we use as proxies for each asset class below.

● **Large Cap Equity (S&P 500)** measures the performance of large capitalization U.S. stocks. The S&P 500 is a market-value-weighted index of 500 stocks. The weightings make each company's influence on the Index performance directly proportional to that company's market value.

● **Small Cap Equity (Russell 2000)** measures the performance of small capitalization U.S. stocks. The Russell 2000 is a market-value-weighted index of the 2,000 smallest stocks in the broad-market Russell 3000 Index.

● **Developed ex-U.S. Equity (MSCI World ex USA)** is an index that is designed to measure the performance of large and mid cap equities in developed markets in Europe, the Middle East, the Pacific region, and Canada.

● **Emerging Market Equity (MSCI Emerging Markets)** is an index that is designed to measure the performance of equity markets in 26 emerging countries around the world.

● **U.S. Fixed Income (Bloomberg Barclays US Aggregate Bond Index)** includes U.S. government, corporate, and mortgage-backed securities with maturities of at least one year.

● **High Yield (Bloomberg Barclays High Yield Bond Index)** measures the market of USD-denominated, non-investment grade, fixed-rate, taxable corporate bonds. Securities are classified as high yield if the middle rating of Moody's, Fitch, and S&P is Ba1/BB+/BB+ or below, excluding emerging market debt.

● **Global ex-U.S. Fixed Income (Bloomberg Barclays Global Aggregate ex US Bond Index)** is an unmanaged index that is comprised of several other Bloomberg Barclays indices that measure the fixed income performance of regions around the world, excluding the U.S.

● **Real Estate (FTSE EPRA Nareit Developed REIT Index)** is designed to measure the stock performance of companies engaged in specific real estate activities in the North American, European, and Asian real estate markets.

● **Cash Equivalent (90-day T-bill)** is a short-term debt obligation backed by the Treasury Department of the U.S. government.

Callan

Callan was founded as an employee-owned investment consulting firm in 1973. Ever since, we have empowered institutional clients with creative, customized investment solutions backed by proprietary research, exclusive data, and ongoing education. Today, Callan advises on more than $2 trillion in total institutional investor assets, which makes it among the largest independently owned investment consulting firms in the U.S. We use a client-focused consulting model to serve pension and defined contribution plan sponsors, endowments, foundations, independent investment advisers, investment managers, and other asset owners. Callan has six offices throughout the U.S. Learn more at www.callan.com.

Corporate Headquarters
San Francisco 800.227.3288

Regional Consulting Offices
Atlanta 800.522.9782
Chicago 800.999.3536
Denver 855.864.3377
Portland, OR 800.227.3268
Summit, NJ 800.274.5878

www.callan.com

owned it every year for twenty years, you would have been on a wild ride. Over the last twenty years large-cap stocks were in the top best performers six times and were the top performer once. But on the downside, they were in the bottom three worst performers six times and at the very bottom once.

The moral to this story is that rather than trying to chase the latest and greatest investment returns, you need to start by understanding and measuring your appetite for risk.

Measuring Your Risk

In a world where thousands of trades can be executed in less than one second, thanks to computer technology, even moves that happened five minutes ago can become old news—and that old news can cost you thousands, if not more, if you haven't diversified your risk.

Right now, because of the market run-up and because of the decade of growth, you're probably taking on far more risk than you realize. We find most families haven't rebalanced their portfolios and diversified their investments. Instead, they've just been on an upward trajectory, and they have far more stocks than they do bonds. Or perhaps they have far more stocks than they do properly diversified funds. You may have thought you were fine when you set your 401(k) contribution ten years ago, and perhaps you've forgotten about it since then.

Bad move.

The reality is that, yes, the growth has been positive for many reasons. However, because of that growth, you're likely taking on higher risk than you can afford.

CASE STUDY: BOB AND CAROL'S RISK PROBLEM

When Bob and Carol came to us, they indicated they weren't comfortable losing more than 10% of the value of their total assets in the case of a market decline.

When we measured their risk, we found that of their $1 million-plus in investments, if the market crashed, they could lose 32% of the value of their investments—or $344,056 of the hard-earned money they'd saved for retirement.

This was a wake-up call for them—and a risk they were not comfortable with so close to retirement.

In Chapter Seven, we will show you how we determined that number for Bob and Carol and how you can find out the same thing about your retirement savings.

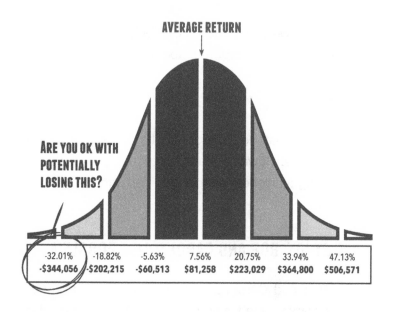

AVERAGE RETURN

ARE YOU OK WITH POTENTIALLY LOSING THIS?

| -32.01% | -18.82% | -5.63% | 7.56% | 20.75% | 33.94% | 47.13% |
| -$344,056 | -$202,215 | -$60,513 | $81,258 | $223,029 | $364,800 | $506,571 |

WHAT'S NEXT?

If you've been approaching your investment and growth strategy in a similar fashion, you could face problems down the line. Bring the conversation back to what matters most to you and to protecting your investment — where egos are out, and your family's best interests are in. You can only get there, though, if you continue being honest about the results of your current growth strategy. Whether you check your 401(k) twice a week or have never once opened a statement, there's time to make a change for the better.

We'll talk about how to do that the right way to approach growth—including how to analyze your risk and understand the value of diversification—in Chapter Seven. Before we get there, though, we have one more stop on our map through the common retirement dilemmas: TAXES.

Everyone's favorite topic—said no one ever!

3

The Tax Dilemma

We grew up in Cottonwood Heights, Utah, about twenty minutes away from some of the world's best ski resorts and surrounded by the incredible Wasatch Mountains. We spent a lot of time in those mountains, and we learned a lot about life living beneath them—it can be a dangerous place to be if you aren't familiar with the threats.

For example, we learned there's almost nothing better than a fresh powder day with all that white, fluffy snow—but we also learned how an amazing snowfall can turn into an avalanche, burying you and possibly even taking your life.

Could your hard-earned savings survive an avalanche of taxes in retirement?

Think back: you may not remember the day exactly, but at one point early in your career, you likely had a conversation with someone from your human resources department. They sat across the table from you and told you all about this great thing called a 401(k), IRA, TSP, 403(b), or 457 — one of several options that make up the alphabet soup of the retirement savings accounts.

They probably told you they were making you a good deal, that putting the money in pre-taxed meant that 100% of your money could grow tax-deferred, which really meant you were saving yourself from paying taxes now in exchange for paying them later. Why was later better? Because, they said, you'd be in a *lower tax bracket*.

A recent article from *Forbes* talks about the exact opposite happening. "Taxes could double in the next ten years...to pay for the ballooning national debt, swollen Social Security and Medicare rolls, etc. For most people, the enormous unfunded liabilities of the federal government, a lot of them linked to the ongoing retirements of the enormous baby boomer generation, is something they don't want to face."[14]

---

14   Larry Light, "Revamping Your Portfolio to Beat the Coming Tax Hikes," *Forbes,* September 30, 2018, https://www.forbes.com/sites/lawrencelight/2018/09/30/revamping-your-portfolio-to-beat-the-coming-tax-hikes/?sh=5df3af22fa19.

The reality of your tax avalanche is that you could be taxed not only on withdrawals from your retirement account, but also on as much as 85% of your Social Security benefit, investment income, estate taxes, and more. When you reach age seventy-two, Uncle Sam will force you to take money out of your retirement account for required minimum distributions (RMDs). If you don't, the penalty is a whopping 50%…one of the highest penalties the IRS can charge you!

What does all this mean to you? If the money you were planning to help you fund your retirement doesn't have a plan for taxes, you could end up with only a fraction of that amount. The avalanche of taxes could not only bury your retirement dreams but kill them altogether!

Will Rogers may have said it best when he quipped, "The only difference between death and taxes is that death doesn't get worse every time Congress meets."

That might make you chuckle, but it's also a hard truth. For most of you…you may be surprised at how bad your tax situation really is. And it could be worse during your retirement years. We can all but guarantee you that you will owe more taxes than you think. Combine that with the fact that government spending is out of control, and it could be a dire combination.

In fact, even with the recent tax cuts in 2017, Bloomberg reported in *InvestmentNews* that Social Security and Medicare are on shaky ground—meaning taxes will likely be raised to accommodate the growing deficit.[15]

Time Magazine reports that "a $2 trillion tax bill is coming due for baby boomers."[16] This report was before the massive stimulus bailout money from the 2020 COVID-19 crisis.

You don't plan and save for retirement your entire adult life only to end up losing it to Uncle Sam, do you? Of course not. That was not your original plan, but it could be your reality if you don't take action.

It's not all doom and gloom, but here's the truth: between the ages of fifty-nine and seventy-two, you have more control over your money than at any time in your life.

We like to say that retirement years are indeed the golden years, but not only for the reasons you may think. They're

---

15   Bloomberg, "Medicare Trust Fund Will Be Exhausted in 2026, Three Years Earlier Than Expected," *InvestmentNews,* June 5, 2018, https://www. investmentnews.com/medicare-trust-fund-will-be-exhausted-in-2026-three-years-earlier-than-expected-74464.

16   Dan Kadlec, "Why a $2 Trillion Tax Bill Is Coming Due for Baby Boomers," *Money,* June 27, 2016, https://money.com/retirement-boomers-taxes-required-withdrawals/.

also golden because we can help you keep the gold in your pocket instead of passing it along to Uncle Sam.

That's right! There is good news: while taxes aren't completely avoidable, if you take action, you might be able to minimize your taxes in retirement. It could put tens of thousands, if not hundreds of thousands, of dollars back in your pocket for retirement.

First, though, you've got to be able to see the avalanche of taxes that could be coming down the mountain, understand how dangerous the avalanche could become... and understand where it could bury you.

THE PROBLEM WITH TAX BUCKET CONFUSION

Have you ever wanted to join a country club? Country clubs were prestigious in the eighties and nineties, right? What if we told you if you don't get your tax strategy ironed out, you could be joining an expensive country club alongside others in your same position? It's one run by Uncle Sam, and you'd be in good company with many other Mr. and Mrs. Double or Triple Taxed couples.

We're joking about the country club, but we're making a serious point. By not having a retirement tax plan, it could needlessly cost you tens of thousands, if not hundreds of thousands, of dollars in taxes.

The system is almost designed that way. For example, there are thousands of pages of tax code. For simplicity, we like to use three buckets to categorize products or investments:

1. Taxed Always (including savings accounts, checking accounts, CDs, etc.)

2. Taxed Later (including 401(k)s, some IRAs, and TSPs—that alphabet soup we mentioned earlier!)

3. Taxed Rarely (including Roth IRAs/401(k)s, life insurance, etc.)

4. The three buckets are ranked good, better, and best—chronologically—for reasons we'll cover

Taxed
Always
(Good)

Taxed
Later
(Better)

Taxed
Rarely
(Best)

in Chapter Nine. For now, it's important to note that too many people focus on bucket two— Taxed Later—because they think it's best to defer taxes.

5. Many families haven't even considered thinking about how to pool money into the best bucket— Taxed Rarely—because they don't know what they don't know. They don't realize they could needlessly pay tens of thousands of dollars, maybe even hundreds of thousands of dollars, in taxes by not realizing what bucket their money has been in all along.

TAX PREPARATION VERSUS TAX PLANNING

Your CPA does tax preparation before every April 15. Makes sense, right? That's his or her job, after all. There are many great CPAs here in Utah and all around the country. There's only one problem you need to consider as you marry your tax strategy to your retirement strategy: most accountants who prepare taxes are looking merely at the past. They focus on the rearview mirror and try to save you tax dollars.

We know what you're thinking: yeah, so what? That's their job.

If you had that thought, you're right. Consider, for a moment, the difference between tax preparation and tax *planning*—and what it could mean to you in the long run. Tax planning means looking ten, twenty, or even thirty years into the future and strategizing on making sure your retirement savings are diversified in the right tax buckets to avoid the avalanche of taxes. It's the difference between being proactive versus reactive. Don't get caught being one of the many that fall into a tax trap that could reduce your retirement savings to just a fraction of what you thought it would be.

With government spending out of control...be honest with yourself: do you think your taxes will be lower or higher in the future? When we ask this question, almost all of our families who meet with us for the first time— those who have worked hard for their money, those who have saved and saved—say their taxes will be higher, yet they're not doing anything to protect themselves against that. In fact, they don't even really understand it. The avalanche of taxes will be a surprise for many as they are clobbered by taxes in retirement.

If that's you, we're going to help. Stick with us.

CASE STUDY:
BOB AND CAROL'S TAX DILEMMA $884,666

*[*Case study is for illustrative purposes only. Results may vary.]*

When Bob and Carol look at where their money is, it is almost all in the "Taxed Later" bucket of 401(k)s and IRAs.

The avalanche of taxes to come on their $1 million is $884,666! How do we know that? We'll show you in Chapter Eight of this book.

WHAT'S NEXT?

You can see that government spending is out of control, and you don't have any control over that. What you do have control over is your own individual tax picture. If you keep your head in the sand and think you can't do anything about taxes in retirement…you could end up in a world of hurt!

If you take action, though, you can be one of the smart and savvy few who pay less—*a lot less*—in taxes because you have a strategy and a plan to get you to and through retirement. In Chapter Eight, we'll show you how to do just that.

Now that you understand that we see the obstacles you're facing in retirement, let's look at what you can do to take action to overcome those obstacles. With a plan and help from experts, you could avoid the nagging pit in your stomach that you could go broke in retirement as your cash runs out and your income sources dry up.

In the next chapter, we're going to ask you to pause and honestly assess where you are and how prepared you are for retirement by completing the B.O.S.S. Retirement Scorecard™. And we want to remind you…as Dan Sullivan says…"All progress starts by telling the truth!"

4

Are You Ready to Retire?

As we were growing up, Dad taught us a valuable lesson from the Memorial Day mudslide at the cabin that we told you about in the introduction of this book. He would often quote Franklin D. Roosevelt: "The only thing to fear is fear itself."

When it came to the Memorial Day mudslide, Dad wasn't going to let that stop him. He always taught us "you can't cry over spilled milk."

Instead of crying about the problem with the cabin, he taught us to get our arms around the problem and look for solutions. To solve any problem, you need to know where you are today by measuring the size of the problem and then have a plan or strategy to get you to where you want to go.

You see, Dad was a barber. He owned a barbershop at Utah's Cottonwood Mall from 1969 to 2006. In the barber chair, Dad would tell his engineer clients about the mudslide problem at the cabin. He would also tell his builder clients about the problem. Then, he'd ask them what they thought he should do.

The engineers taught him how to measure if the cabin was moving and then how to stabilize the foundation. The builders told him how he needed to jack up the cabin to square up the foundation.

From there, Dad used his new system to measure the cabin movement every spring to check and make sure there was no movement from year to year in the foundation. After a couple years of measuring, he decided to take the next step of squaring up the cabin.

First, he took the engineer's advice and jackhammered six large holes into the foundation of the cabin. He drilled down deep and added pylons deep into the mountain to stabilize the foundation.

Then, using what he had learned from the builders, he brought in house jacks and lifted the cabin up to make it square. Then, he brought in a massive beam and set it on large logs and created a new foundation support structure wall on the back of the cabin.

Since that day, the cabin has not moved at all. We hope it stays that way for decades to come. We've made lots of great family memories there, like barbeques on Memorial Day, homemade ice cream, and lots of kids and grand-kids enjoying spending time with each other.

Years later, we would use these same principles to measure and improve thousands of families' retirement plans with what we call the B.O.S.S. Retirement Score-card™ and the B.O.S.S. Retirement Blueprint™.

THE B.O.S.S. RETIREMENT SCORECARD™

We developed the B.O.S.S. Retirement Scorecard™—a simple two-page self-evaluation tool to measure your retirement readiness. The first page of the scorecard is to help you measure where you are today. Page two of the scorecard will help you get clarity on what dangers you feel you have and then clarity on what you want for your retirement.

Before we have you start on page one of the scorecard, answer this question:

On a percentage scale of one to one hundred, what percent would you give yourself on how prepared you are for retirement?

A score of 1% is you have not started. A score of 100% is you are perfect and have no room for improvement.

Write your score here: _____

Next, find the B.O.S.S. Retirement Scorecard™ in chapter 4. The B.O.S.S. Retirement Scorecard™ is based on the eight mindsets we have found that build a successful retirement. Be honest with yourself. Remember, all progress starts by telling the truth!

Here are the eight mindsets we will measure:

1. Debt

2. Cash

3. Income/Inflation

4. Social Security

5. Growth/Investments

6. Taxes

7. Healthcare/Long-Term Care

8. Legacy

For each category, you will score your own retirement readiness, following the clearly defined ranking system. For each section, a rank of one is the lowest in terms of readiness, and a rank of twelve is the highest.

It's important to note that there is no perfect score. The point is to be brutally honest as you grade yourself. Use this exercise to tell yourself the truth. Remember, you can't cry over spilled milk (past losses). Don't try to sugarcoat this. Be honest with yourself because your future retirement could depend on it.

For example, say you find yourself with middle scores in some areas. Perhaps you know your score in the Growth/Investments section—the column that says "have a 401(k) or not sure how to invest for growth"—but you don't know whether to mark four, five, or six. Ask yourself how you feel and go with your gut.

B.O.S.S. RETIREMENT SCORECARD™

MINDSETS	1	2	3	4	5	6
1 Debt	You are only paying minimum payments on all your credit cards, auto loans, and mortgage.			You are paying some principal on credit cards, auto loans, and mortgage.		
2 Cash	In the hole every month. Your expenses are more than your income. You have to borrow from credit cards to live each month.			You are trying to get out of debt. You have no emergency fund.		
3 Income/Inflation	You have no retirement income plan. You worry about where your next check will come from when you retire.			You recognize that your Social Security is the foundation of your income plan.		
4 Social Security	You don't know if you even qualify for Social Security. You are not sure where you can find competent advice.			You take Social Security at face value and listen to your friends and family to find out general rules of thumb on Social Security.		
5 Growth/ Retirement Investments	You have no investments.			You have a 401K. You're not sure what else you have or how to start investing.		
6 Taxes	You think there is no way to change your tax situation. You are not organized and every year tax time is stressful for you.			All of your investment accounts are taxable as earned. Most of your money is in the bank or investment brokerage accounts.		
7 Health Care/ Long Term Care	You have no plan and no Health Insurance. A serious medical emergency will wipe you out financially.			You have a basic Health Insurance Plan that has high deductibles and covers you only for catastrophic medical care.		
8 Legacy	You have no plan to transfer your assets to those you love. You always worry when you travel. You believe it will be a disaster if you die.			You have a basic Will but it is not updated and your beneficiaries are not clearly designated.		
RETIREMENT READINESS SCORE →			→	→	→	

7	8	9	10	11	12	SCORE
You are paying down principal balances on debt payments and have a plan and a date of when your debt free.			You have less than 24 months of payments left on all debt payments. You will be debt free before you retire.			
You have started saving but you have less than 6 months saved in your emergency fund.			You have saved 6 months of emergency funds. You have saved sufficient funds to help you feel confident in surviving any emergency that comes your way.			
You have Social Security payment(s) plus one additional reliable income source that is not dependent upon the stock market.			You have a plan to optimize Social Security and you have at least two additional reliable income sources that are not dependent upon the stock market.			
You have researched Social Security on the internet but are still afraid of making mistakes. You are not confident in which option is best.			You understand the difference between optimizing and maximizing your Social Security and have it built into the rest of your plan.			
You are investing but money keeps going up and down. You don't understand and you have no plan to protect yourself.			You have a plan to reduce risk and beat inflation. You have confidence in a down market.			
You understand the power of taxed later accounts like a 401K or IRA. You have no plan on how to minimize taxes on these accounts.			You have proper tax diversification and your investments grow tax free and will distributed tax free. You have Roth and Life Insurance.			
You have a basic Health Insurance Plan and a plan for Medicare and Medicare supplements.			You have a comprehensive plan which includes: Health Insurance, Medicare, Medicare Supplements, Life, and Long Term Care.			
You have a Will, Trust, Financial and Medical Directives but they are out of date and do not reflect your current wishes.			Your Will, Trust, Financial and Medical Directive are all current. Your money will stay in the family and not to the government.			
→ → → → → → → → → → →						

We find most people score in the range of the fifties to seventies when they complete their scorecard. Even if you score a twelve in each of the eight areas, you'll have a score of ninety-six. In other words, there is no perfect retirement plan—no 100% because Social Security may change, investment options will change based on market conditions, and taxes, including estate plan rules, will likely change from one administration to another in the future.

The goal of this exercise is to give you a clear picture of where you are, and we can help you get where you want to go. It doesn't matter what your score is today so long as you are committed to improving and making your retirement plan better tomorrow than it was today.

Take ten minutes, right now, and take the assessment. Sit at your table and gather all the resources you need to answer the questions honestly. Do you have a small 401(k) from a job you held years ago that you've never done anything with? Do you have a business that will generate monthly income, but you aren't sure of its sustainability as you get closer to retirement?

Think of your financial history as a puzzle—which, for many of our clients, isn't far from the truth. You have decades of decisions you have made that have gotten you to this point, after all.

We aren't asking you to put your puzzle together right now; we will help with that in Part II. Instead, right now, we want you to simply put it all on the table—literally. Make sure all the pieces are in one spot so we can build together.

Your future self will thank you!

What was your Retirement Readiness Score?

Write your Retirement Readiness Score here: _____

How does your score compare with your first answer? Before: _____ After: _____

B.O.S.S. Retirement Scorecard™ Page Two: Making Your Future Better Than Your Past

What do you want in retirement?

What legacy do you want to leave to those you love or your favorite charity?

What obstacles are stopping you from getting what you want?

This is where planning for retirement gets exciting! Often you are so busy with life you don't take the time to get clarity on what matters most to you and create a vision for retirement.

When you think of retiring, you may be tempted to only think in dollars and cents. However, the key to making your retirement future bigger than your past is to have purpose in your planning, based on what you see as the dangers or obstacles that create worries about retiring, and clarity on what you want your retirement to look like.

Page two of the B.O.S.S. Retirement Scorecard™ gives you a chance to write down your dangers or worries and set your retirement vision by writing down what you want. We invite you to ponder the following question and write down the answers in each area of your scorecard.

The R-Factor Questions®[17]: If we were sitting here three years from today, looking back on today, what would have to happen for you to be happy with your progress, both personally and with your retirement?

We invite you to spend the next ten minutes writing this down. If you are married, do this with your partner.

---

17   *The R-Factor Question® is a tool created and owned by Strategic Coach.*

DREAM BIG and don't worry about justifying why you want what you want...just get it down on paper.

In the "What Do I Have" section of the scorecard, write down all of the resources and assets you have for retirement. This does not need to be down to the penny, just the approximate value to help you see your strengths and what you have done to this point to save for retirement.

Now let's check in with Bob and Carol to see how they scored and what they wrote down!

CASE STUDY:
BOB AND CAROL'S SCORECARD SCORE

Bob and Carol felt pretty good about retirement because they had saved $1 million for retirement. Before completing the B.O.S.S. Retirement Scorecard™, they thought they were 80% prepared to retire. After completing the assessment, they realized there were more areas they were not confident in and were surprised when their Retirement Readiness Score was a sixty-one, but they felt that was accurate after being honest with themselves and discussing it as a couple.

On the vision page of their scorecard they found it exciting to get clarity on what their concerns were and what

B.O.S.S. RETIREMENT SCORECARD™

DANGERS: **WHAT I WORRY ABOUT**

1.
2.
3.
4.
5.

RETIREMENT VISION: **WHAT I WANT**

1.
2.
3.
4.
5.

0%   50%   100%

RETIREMENT STRENGTHS

WHAT DO I HAVE?

Cash $	☐ Yes	☐ No	Other Income $	☐ Yes	☐ No
Social Security $	☐ Yes	☐ No	401(k) / IRA $	☐ Yes	☐ No
Pension $	☐ Yes	☐ No	Real Estate $	☐ Yes	☐ No

B.O.S.S. RETIREMENT SCORECARD™

DANGERS: **WHAT I WORRY ABOUT**

1. Will Social Security be there?
2. Running out of money
3. Stock market crash
4. Pay too much in taxes
5. No will or trust

RETIREMENT VISION: **WHAT I WANT**

1. Time with kids & grandkids
2. More time to paint
3. Hunt & fish more
4. Serve in community
5. Peace of mind – have a plan

0%   50%   100%

RETIREMENT STRENGTHS

WHAT DO I HAVE?

Cash $ 60,000	☒ Yes	☐ No	Other Income $ 0	☐ Yes	☒ No
Social Security $?	☒ Yes	☐ No	401(k) / IRA $ 1,074,838	☒ Yes	☐ No
Pension $ 0	☐ Yes	☒ No	Real Estate $ 450,000	☒ Yes	☐ No

they wanted in retirement. Let's look at Bob and Carol's B.O.S.S. Retirement Scorecard™ to see how they evaluated themselves.

WHAT'S NEXT?

If your dream retirement is your destination, you need a blueprint to help you on your journey. In this chapter, you've used the retirement scorecard to outline your starting point—the X that says, "you are here."

As you can imagine, the way forward is far from a straight line. You'll face challenges along the way, but you'll make smarter decisions and be better prepared if you're educated about what the trek will entail. Just like the mudslide at the cabin.

In Part II, we'll reveal the B.O.S.S. Retirement Blueprint™ and offer solutions and tools to help you generate and keep the momentum you need to reach your retirement goals and dreams.

Ready, set, go!

Building Your Optimal System of Security for Retirement

5

The B.O.S.S.
Retirement
Blueprint™

The very first time we sought our own financial plan, we met with an advisor—one we were told was one of the best in his field. Before he would tell us anything, he asked us each to write him a check for $3,500…each!

That sounded reasonable at the time. After all, the planning process was going to be a lot of work, right? In the end, for $7,000 total, we received a binder of ninety-three pages of boilerplate nonsense. We couldn't decipher it, it was overwhelming, and, as a result, it was of little value to our future retirement. So, we did what most people do in situations like this: we stuck it on the bookshelf— nothing but a very expensive, non-personalized pile of paper—and never looked at it again.

When we started our firm, one of our goals was to provide the opposite approach and change millions of lives. We wanted to do that by providing massive value upfront to our clients. We believe that if we give good information to good people, together we can make great decisions for their retirement.

What we got from that advisor is the opposite of what our plan, the B.O.S.S. Retirement Blueprint™, offers: one page of customization and simplicity. And, as Leonardo da Vinci said, "Simplicity is the ultimate in sophistication."

Da Vinci wasn't alone in appreciating the value of simple solutions. In the early nineteenth century, William of Occam proposed a rule for science and philosophy alike that essentially states the following: if there are competing explanations or theories for some phenomenon, always prefer the simplest one. This rule of preferring simplicity became known as Occam's razor. Staying true to the spirit of this principle, the B.O.S.S. Retirement Blueprint™ helps you gain control of your own situation.

Even—and, we'd argue, especially—in modern times, simplicity most often wins. But it can be hard to let go of what things were like before. You may have been working with your financial advisor for ten, fifteen, or even twenty years at this point.

Our good friend Dan Sullivan reminds us of a story, though, about change: in the Book of Exodus in the Bible, Moses leads the children of Israel out of Egypt. Later in the story, he says, "The skills and tools that got you out of Egypt are not the same skills and tools that will get you to the Promised Land."

If you're looking for the promised land of retirement, you may think you're on a path there—you may have your own binder on your own shelf, gathering dust—but we have learned after meeting with thousands of clients that you most likely don't have a written plan for your journey to the retirement promised land.

As one study found, "Most Americans spend less time planning for an IRA investment for their retirement than they do choosing a restaurant, flat screen TV, or tablet."[18]

---

18   "TIAA-CREF Survey Finds Americans Spend Less Time Planning Their IRA Investment Than Choosing a Restaurant," *TIAA*, March 13, 2014, https://www.tiaa.org/public/about-tiaa/news-press/press-releases/pressrelease495.html.

In fact, fewer than 25% of pre-retirees have a plan for retirement, and—as we've seen—those who do often don't customize them.[19]

So, our question to you is this…do you have a plan that's custom-tailored to your situation? More than anything, you need simplicity and clarity so you can have confidence that you won't hit the pitfalls and fall through the trapdoors we mentioned in Part I of this book. Don't let a lack of preparedness rob you of your retirement. The B.O.S.S. Retirement Blueprint™ is here to help.

B.O.S.S. RETIREMENT BLUEPRINT™ = VISION

We carefully designed the one-page B.O.S.S. Retirement Blueprint™ so you can see the big picture in its simplest form. The blueprint gives you a vision of where you are and where you want to go in retirement to feel happy with your progress.

The blueprint focuses on the retirement fundamentals in the form of five buckets: cash, income, growth, taxes, and legacy.

---

19   "Most Americans Don't Have a Financial Plan, and Many Think Their Wealth Doesn't Deserve One," *Business Wire,* May 15, 2018, https://www.businesswire.com/news/home/20180515005598/en/Americans-Don%E2%80%99t-Financial-Plan-Wealth-Doesn%E2%80%99t-Deserve.

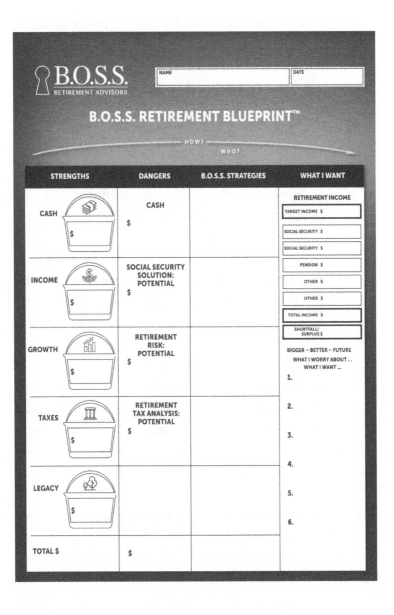

B.O.S.S. RETIREMENT BLUEPRINT™

HOW?
WHO?

STRENGTHS	DANGERS	B.O.S.S. STRATEGIES	WHAT I WANT
CASH $	CASH $		RETIREMENT INCOME
INCOME $	SOCIAL SECURITY SOLUTION: POTENTIAL $		TARGET INCOME $
GROWTH $	RETIREMENT RISK: POTENTIAL $		SOCIAL SECURITY $
TAXES $	RETIREMENT TAX ANALYSIS: POTENTIAL $		SOCIAL SECURITY $
LEGACY $			PENSION $
TOTAL $	$		OTHER $

RETIREMENT INCOME

TARGET INCOME $

SOCIAL SECURITY $

SOCIAL SECURITY $

PENSION $

OTHER $

OTHER $

TOTAL INCOME $

SHORTFALL/ SURPLUS $

BIGGER – BETTER – FUTURE
WHAT I WORRY ABOUT ...
WHAT I WANT ...

1.

2.

3.

4.

5.

6.

In this section of the book, we'll follow the blueprint starting at the top and going to the bottom. If you can master these five buckets, you will find this one-page blueprint could help you navigate most challenges you will face in retirement.

Note that this is not a one-size-fits-all solution. Why? Those don't exist. They end up much like our first plan...as binders on the shelf that you never pick up again. Small changes in your age, health, Social Security distributions, pension amounts, income sources—small details in each of these areas can swing a big hinge on where you go and how you get there. What you need is a simple plan to help you reach that dream retirement you thought about when you first picked up this book—and this is the tool to make it happen.

With each bucket, it's important to be honest with yourself—just like you were when filling out your scorecard. Start by taking the things you have as your retirement strengths and do your best to put an amount you have available in each bucket.

Let's get real. You may be embarrassed because you feel like you haven't saved enough. Are you feeling like you've lost hope after reading about the retirement dilemmas in Part I?

It's okay. If we're going to make progress, we need a truthful analysis of where we are—the good and the not-so-good.

Start by gathering your cash bucket information. In the remaining pages of this book, we'll progress through the other four buckets as well.

A CLOSER LOOK AT THE CASH BUCKET

Let's take the first step on the blueprint and determine how much money you want to have set aside in cash for an emergency if something unexpected happens. We call this the cash bucket. You can refer back to the B.O.S.S. Retirement Scorecard™ to help you determine how much you want to set aside here. Let's go!

How did you rank yourself? Are you a two on the scorecard, who is in the hole every month, borrowing from credit cards to make it by? Maybe you're a six, with no savings to speak of? An eight with some savings, but not enough to be entirely confident? An eleven with six months of emergency funds?

Six months of funds—a ten to twelve on your scorecard—is the ideal. That way, you can have confidence you can survive an emergency.

CASE STUDY:
BOB AND CAROL'S SCORECARD

Currently, Bob and Carol came to us with a cash ranking of ten on their scorecard. They thought a figure of $60,000 in savings was great—and it was, of course. But, ten years ago, Bob was laid off from his job and didn't sleep well at night.

We spoke with them, and together, we decided their sleep-well-at-night number should be $75,000, to give them peace of mind that they could cover any unexpected expenses. When a retirement plan is designed for Bob and Carol, planning should be completed to increase their cash bucket savings from $60,000 up to $75,000. This can be accomplished by saving more each month or reallocating current investments to have more in cash to help them sleep better at night.

STRENGTHS	DANGERS	B.O.S.S. STRATEGIES
CASH $ 60,000	CASH $	INCREASE CASH BUCKET TO $75,000

WHAT'S NEXT?

In the following chapters, we'll examine how the other buckets on the B.O.S.S. Retirement Blueprint™ of income, growth, taxes and legacy will help you overcome the challenges we discussed in Part I of this book as tools to further guide you on your journey.

Now is where the real journey begins! Do you remember when we told you the three most important words in retirement were "income, income, income?" Let's aim for the center of that income bullseye and identify where your income will come from in retirement!

6

The Income Solution

If you stopped working today, how much reliable retirement income would you need to pay for your lifestyle each month? Really think about it…if you spend $7,500 per month or $90,000 per year, where will that money come from each month?

Go ahead…add it all up. In most cases it doesn't take long because for most Americans, the only source of reliable retirement income is Social Security!

In today's social media–driven world of trying to make your life look perfect, everybody wants to talk about and show you their perfect life. We call them your shining moments that do happen in life, but they are usually the exception and not the rule of what your daily life is really like.

Examples could be sharing photos of your dream vacation with perfectly posed, happy, smiling children...or publicly posting when you did something to serve your neighbor so you can be seen and admired by friends and neighbors as a good guy or gal and feel better about yourself.

Few like to be vulnerable and talk about their worst days...

How do we know this? Firsthand...from real-life experience in the school of hard knocks where the school colors are...black and blue! We've also helped thousands of people just like you retire, so we can help you customize a strategy that works for your goals.

If we want to make real progress with our retirement, we need to be honest with ourselves and talk about the dark moments as well as the shining moments! The darkest moments are usually the best teachers if we can learn from the mistakes and not repeat them.

Before we talk about your income in retirement, let us tell you about a time when our income stopped. It is a painful memory...it is a very dark moment that we hope you can learn from, and we hope that you won't repeat the same mistakes we made! Let's get in the time machine and see how we learned the importance of reliable income firsthand!

BUSINESS FAILURE, FORECLOSURES, SHORT SALES...OH MY!

Growing up as the fifth and sixth children of seven, lots of thing went right for us. We had a "perfect life checklist," and we were checking things off that list with the best of them. We were Eagle Scouts, started our first business when we were in high school, served two-year missions for our church, and, while in college, the business we started in high school paid us more money than what most starting salaries were for post-grads.

Life was exciting! As we graduated, a friend introduced us to the mortgage banking business, and we saw the small company we worked for grow from one office to over twenty! That business then sold to a national company, and we had our first front-row seat watching an American success story grow and develop!

After that company sold, we got on board with another small mortgage bank, and we helped it grow from less than twenty employees to over six hundred and become a dominant player in the mortgage industry.

Everything felt like it was going perfectly! Income? Boy, we had it. We were maxing out our 401(k)s, buying investment real estate, and thinking we had the world by the tail. We were living the "perfect" life.

After watching two businesses experience exponential growth, we decided it was time for us to own our own company again. In 2001, we formed a real estate investment and development company, leveraging all the knowledge and networks we had, and for the next six years hit a home run in one of the best real estate markets in history.

In the spring of 2007, with everyone and their neighbor doing a real estate deal, we decided to cash out of our real estate portfolio. Hindsight being 20/20, we later realized that it was almost perfect timing to avoid the coming real estate meltdown! Again, we timed it right and avoided the pain of the Great Recession real estate crash.

By spring of 2007, we cashed out our real estate portfolio except for some income producing properties, and we thought life could not be much better—at only thirty-four and thirty-two years old, we felt like we were on top of the world!

They say that "pride cometh before the fall." Well, at this moment, we felt like Midas, and everything we had

touched to this point in our lives had turned to gold. But a big lesson was waiting just around the Great Recession corner!

We thought we had the world by the tail, so we figured it would be okay to take some time off and decide what we wanted our next venture to be. For a little over a year, we looked for a problem we could solve, and, ultimately, we decided to start a business helping thirty- to forty-year-olds plan and prepare for retirement.

From our time in the mortgage industry, we observed that thirty- to forty-year-olds weren't paying attention to their retirement because they were too burdened by their credit cards, auto loans, mortgage payments, etc.; in short, on average, 30%–40% of their gross income was going to pay for debt.

They had no retirement savings. At retirement, they would end up like most Americans, hoping that Social Security would be there to pay the bills, or they would take the alternative route...living in their kid's basement.

We had a deep desire to help, so we built a business to do just that. The business goal was to help millions of thirty- to forty-year-olds get a head start on their retirement by quickly paying off their debts, saving more each month, and preparing so that when they got to retirement, they would have the assets to be financially secure and independent.

Sounds like a great business, right? There was no way it could fail, right? We thought we had the next American success story, and we launched the company in 2008— right at the beginning of the Great Recession!

Here is one game-changing memory about this time that is fresh in our minds to this day: it was September 2008, and we had just taken our families to Disneyland. Walking through the lobby of our hotel, we saw the headline: "Lehman Brothers Declares Bankruptcy."

Shocked that one of the crown jewels of Wall Street had just failed, we looked at each other and said, "This is not going to be good." We were right...it was not good, and we were about to learn a very hard lesson!

Fast forward two years, and the dream of helping thirty- to forty-year-old individuals and families prepare for retirement had turned into our own personal nightmare! By September 2010, we'd burned through all our personal and business cash savings. Still believing we could make it work, we leveraged our remaining income-producing rental properties to keep the dream alive.

We were all in...100% committed to making this work! We put all we had financially, emotionally, and physically into the business. But in the end, despite giving everything we had to this dream...this business model failed!

We had to face the hard reality that the dream was over! We were forced to let go of all our employees, and, to make matters worse, we faced a crushing mountain of debt.

We'd gone from having more success than we'd ever dreamed to being in business debt to the tune of over $3.1 million. And the real problem...we had a failed business model with no income to pay that debt back to our creditors!

Our attorneys and advisors told us it was time to declare bankruptcy and start over. They could see no possible way we could get out of this mess. In reality, we could not see a way to get out of this mess!

This was a turning point for us in our lives. To get clarity, we went to the family cabin, and for a week we shut out the world and the terrible challenges we were facing. We faced our fear head-on by making a list of every debt we owed and every problem we faced.

We prayed with more intensity than we had ever prayed before, and we asked God if it was right that we should declare bankruptcy. From a common-sense logical approach, it made sense to us, but we wanted to know if that is what God wanted for us.

As is often the case, "Man's ways are not God's ways." In short…his answer surprised us…

After telling God we had made the decision to declare bankruptcy and asking him for his confirmation on that decision, his response was crystal clear…

No, he did not want us to declare bankruptcy. He wanted us to pay ALL OF OUR DEBTS!

And so, we did…

We followed God's direction, and in about a two-year period, we paid off or settled all $3.1 million in business debt without declaring bankruptcy!

But make no mistake, these were some of the darkest days of our lives and included foreclosure of rental properties, short sells, and battling with creditors daily to pay off the debt while at the same time trying to provide a way to have enough income to provide for our young families.

That experience was literal deliverance for us and our families. No different than the waters parting for the children of Israel to flee from Pharaoh's army, we were delivered from a mountain of debt!

What did we learn from this experience? And how does it relate to your retirement?

Lesson One: Life is no fun when you have a mountain of debt and no income, just like retirement without reliable retirement income is not fun and doesn't work!

Lesson Two: For your retirement to be a success, it must be based on INCOME and NOT assets! It is not how much you have saved; it is how much income you have to pay for your lifestyle. The more income you have, the more abundant retirement lifestyle you can enjoy!

Lesson Three: Most thirty- to forty-year-olds are NOT focused on retirement. Most are more interested in a new house, a new car, and taking their kids to Disneyland than they are about preparing for a successful retirement. You may have been like that in your thirties and forties, and that is why you are now wondering how you are going to make it through retirement.

Lesson Four: The fifty-five- to seventy-year-olds are VERY concerned about retirement. This is probably why you are reading this book right now. Good news: we can help you!

Our failed business model didn't work because, at the end of the day, thirty- to forty-year-olds simply aren't focused enough on retirement. They needed our help, but they didn't want our help.

More importantly, we owned *OUR* mistake: we had little income coming in during that time. We were depleting our entire savings trying to grow the business. We learned that one of the fastest ways we know of to run out of money in retirement is to start retirement without an income plan and live off your savings.

That's why we repeat the same phrase over and over to our clients:

In your retirement, the three most important words are income, income, income.

This painful experience drove that point home, and—like most great lessons—it helped us to become better retirement planners. Not only did it help us to be more compassionate as we help people with their retirements, but it helped us learn firsthand the importance of having multiple streams coming into your retirement bucket so that your retirement reservoir doesn't run dry, like ours did.

Now, let's talk about how this applies to your retirement. We will start with the foundation of your retirement income: Social Security!

HOW DO YOU WRING EVERY NICKEL OUT OF YOUR SOCIAL SECURITY BENEFITS?

We're going to start with your Social Security benefits—and for good reason. You've been paying into Social Security for the last twenty, thirty, maybe even forty years or more. That means 12.4% of every paycheck that you've *ever* earned throughout your lifetime—going back to the first one you earned as a kid—has gone into Social Security.

Rightfully, it's the foundation of your income plan, and it's our job to help you wring every nickel and dime out of the program that is rightfully yours.

We find many families rely on Social Security as their sole source of income during retirement—something

we clearly don't recommend. However, it happens. The Social Security Administration website states: "Social Security benefits are the most widely received source of income among Americans aged sixty-five or older, and they are the largest source of income for more than half of aged beneficiaries (Social Security Administration [SSA] 2014)."[20]

Whether you use Social Security as your primary source of income or you have several streams coming in (the

---

20   https://www.ssa.gov/policy/docs/ssb/v75n3/v75n3p15.html.

best-case scenario), your relationship in taking Social Security is the same: it's a foundational piece of your income strategy, and you want to build your foundation as strong as possible.

As we mentioned in Chapter Two, there are over 2,278 rules in the Social Security handbook, and even one wrong choice could cost you big in the long run. We help simplify Social Security for our clients by providing a customized Social Security analysis and guide them to the most beneficial choices for their age and situation. In our analysis, we even include a glossary of key terms so that the material is understandable and more than a complicated boilerplate retirement binder.

The B.O.S.S. Social Security Solution™ accomplishes five main goals, helping you to know:

- How and when to claim your benefit so you get the highest return.

- How to minimize and even elimi-
nate paying taxes on as much as 85%
of your Social Security benefit.

- How to avoid possibly doubling or even
tripling your Medicare premium.

- How you can use one simple trick to
  maximize your spousal benefit.

- How to find other additional benefits that are rightfully yours.

Along the way, you'll also discover customized advice
on how to:

- Pick your starting age on your own monthly
  benefit, as well as, if you are married,
  the most beneficial decision for your
  spouse and their spousal benefit.

- A primary and secondary strategy for withdrawal (and the implications of each).

- A discussion of protection against longevity risk.

- Important information about critical filing dates.

- An overview of the annual benefits you
  can expect, and at what age.

- An overview of your annual expenses in
  relation to your benefits, per year.

- A recap of why the strategy recommended is best for your situation—in plain English.

- A discussion of taxes and how they relate to your Social Security.

- An analysis of your cumulative lifetime Social Security benefits.

- A break-even analysis on both the primary and secondary strategies recommended.

- A projection of potential healthcare costs in retirement and a related discussion of Medicare costs and benefits.

- A discussion of the importance of considering long-term care in your retirement.

- And more.[21]

---

21   If you reach out to us and mention that you've read this book and understand why Social Security is an important part of income in retirement, we'll run a Social Security analysis for you—for free.

Case Study: The B.O.S.S. Social Security Solution™ for Bob and Carol

For Bob and Carol, a closer look at their Social Security strategy shows you how to avoid leaving tens of thousands, if not hundreds of thousands, of dollars on the table when you claim your benefits. After reviewing their customized Social Security analysis, Bob and Carol could see all the options available to them, and we helped them optimize the best timing for their situation.

At the end of the day, after creating a customized plan, we came up with a strategy that could optimize Bob and Carol's Social Security payout up to a whopping *$100,163!*

STRENGTHS	DANGERS	B.O.S.S. STRATEGIES
INCOME	SOCIAL SECURITY SOLUTION: POTENTIAL $ 100,163	OPTIMIZE SOCIAL SECURITY PAYOUT

What would you do with an extra $100,163 in your pocket during retirement? That is money that could help you pay off debt, travel, or spend more time with kids and grandkids!

What about My Pension Income?

If you have a pension, consider yourself one of the lucky roughly one out of five people today who has a pension to count as an income stream. If so, that's what we typically consider a second source of reliable retirement income.

Your decision of how and when to take your pension is also a big decision you should consider before you retire. Unfortunately, when you retire, you'll likely face a human resources representative who will push a piece of paper in front of you that may be confusing because it is full of options for how you can take your pension.

Do you take the biggest number that you can receive monthly (for life), but if you die, nothing goes to a surviving spouse? If you're married, should you consider what percentage of your pension goes to a surviving spouse? Is it 50%, 75%, or 100%? You need to realize that the closer to 100% that is given to the surviving spouse, the less money you'll be entitled to each month.

All these considerations, of course, are only valid if the company pension fund remains viable. Are you worried about your pension fund lasting as long as you do? In fact, *Business Insider* reports that the US pension system has gotten so bad that Congress is already planning for its failure. The article states, "The Pension Guarantee Corporation, the equivalent of the FDIC, is completely insolvent."[22]

So, should you take a lump sum out at retirement so that you can be in control of your hard-earned money? Or should you hang in there and take the monthly benefit and cross your fingers that the pension funds will last? How do you avoid losing money in the form of fees to the pension fund managers...and how do you minimize your taxes when you combine your pension income with your Social Security income? These are all important questions to ask yourself before you retire. It's all got to be part of your plan.

What Other Options Are There to Generate Income in Retirement?

If you're not one of the roughly one in five people who has a pension, you already know Social Security is not likely to cover all your income needs in retirement. So how will YOU generate reliable retirement income from your retirement savings?

---

22   Simon Black, "The US Pension System Has Gotten So Bad That Congress Is Planning for Its Failure." *Business Insider*, March 22, 2018, https://www.businessinsider.com/us-pension-policy-is-so-bad-that-congress-is-planning-for-its-failure-2018-3.

Unfortunately, today it has become harder than ever to generate income in retirement. With record-low interest rates on savings accounts and CDs...it makes it nearly impossible to retire off your hard-earned savings. Bonds aren't much better, and the volatility of the stock market makes it difficult to predict how much income to take from your investment accounts.

Regardless of what income streams you personally choose, we recommend you have at least three so that your retirement reservoir doesn't run dry.

- Let's take a look at some of the other traditional ways to generate retirement income in retirement. **Bank savings and CDs.** Do you remember the interest rates of the 1980s? Back then, you'd get double digit rates on savings accounts and CD accounts—but it's not the 1980s. Today, it's a whole new ball game. Rates on savings accounts and CDs are a joke. It's more like 1% instead of 12%. For example, in the good old days you could place your money in a bank CD and make a 12% income. That means if Bob and Carol were to put their $1 million in investable savings into a CD, they'd generate $120,000 in interest annually or $10,000 per month without touching the principal. At the time of this writing, though, interest rates are down to around

1%-2%. At 1%, that's only $10,000 per year or $833 per month! To make matters worse, they'd still need to pay taxes on that low return!

- **Dividend-paying stocks.** Some well-known, established brands such as Coca-Cola have a history of paying out a dividend on their stocks that you can turn into income. Dividends can be a great source of retirement income, but we recommend having a professional determine what companies you should consider for reliable dividends or selecting a dividend fund that provides a portfolio of dividend-paying companies.

- **Annuities.** Annuities could provide a way to create reliable retirement income or safe growth that locks in gains and does not lose value in a stock market downturn, but you still need the help of an expert before you consider any annuity options. Annuities are full of landmines. In fact, 90%-95% of them are not suitable for you to put your money into. Immediate annuities, fixed annuities, variable annuities, or fixed indexed annuities all have their pros and cons, but you should understand what you are buying before you select one of them.

- **Bonds.** Bond interest rates are very low…in fact, bonds are hardly paying anything as of this writing—but, that said, remember that the point is diversification. They may still be a viable option as a part of your plan both now and in the future.

- **Real estate.** Perhaps **you've a**cquired some real estate over the course of your career. If so, the monthly rental income from real estate can help fill your income bucket. On the other hand, maybe you've decided you no longer want to fix toilets as you head into retirement. One option to consider is having your real estate managed by a property manager, and another option is to invest in a real estate fund.

Should You Worry About Inflation?

A general rule of thumb is that whatever you're spending today—keeping in mind the one-hundred-year historical average of inflation—you're going to need to double it every twenty years just to keep up with inflation. If you need $5,000 today for retirement, your plan should include a strategy to receive $10,000 per month twenty years down the road to cover normal increases in inflation.

Case Study: Bob and Carol's Retirement Income Analysis

Coming back to Bob and Carol's case, their B.O.S.S. Retirement Blueprint™ income analysis shows they were spending $5,000 per month, and that's what they would need to maintain their lifestyle when they retire. As a result of inflation, by the time they retire, we project that they will actually need $5,830.

Starting with Social Security, we determine that Bob will receive $2,975 and Carol will receive $1,968, for a total of $4,943. This will result in a shortfall of $887 in income per month.

Retirement income need: $5,830

Social Security income: $4,943

Shortfall: ($887)/month

WHAT I WANT

RETIREMENT INCOME

TARGET INCOME $	5,830

SOCIAL SECURITY $	2,975
SOCIAL SECURITY $	1,968
PENSION $	
OTHER $	
OTHER $	

TOTAL INCOME $	4,943

SHORTFALL/ SURPLUS $	-887

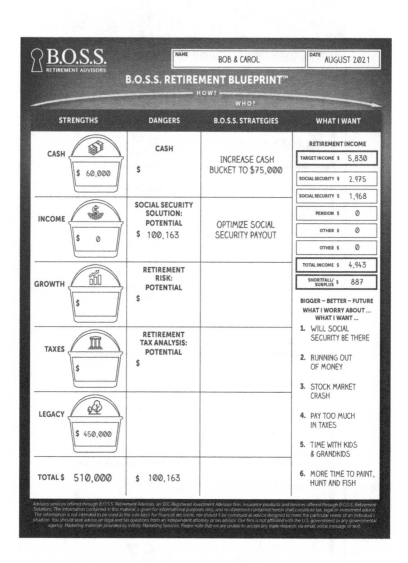

	STRENGTHS	DANGERS	B.O.S.S. STRATEGIES	WHAT I WANT

B.O.S.S. RETIREMENT BLUEPRINT™

NAME: BOB & CAROL
DATE: AUGUST 2021

HOW?
WHO?

STRENGTHS	DANGERS	B.O.S.S. STRATEGIES
CASH $ 60,000	**CASH** $	INCREASE CASH BUCKET TO $75,000
INCOME $ 0	**SOCIAL SECURITY SOLUTION: POTENTIAL** $ 100,163	OPTIMIZE SOCIAL SECURITY PAYOUT
GROWTH $	**RETIREMENT RISK: POTENTIAL** $	
TAXES $	**RETIREMENT TAX ANALYSIS: POTENTIAL** $	
LEGACY $ 450,000		
TOTAL $ 510,000	$ 100,163	

WHAT I WANT

RETIREMENT INCOME

TARGET INCOME $	5,830
SOCIAL SECURITY $	2,975
SOCIAL SECURITY $	1,968
PENSION $	0
OTHER $	0
OTHER $	0
TOTAL INCOME $	4,943
SHORTFALL/ SURPLUS $	887

BIGGER – BETTER – FUTURE
WHAT I WORRY ABOUT ...
WHAT I WANT ...

1. WILL SOCIAL SECURITY BE THERE
2. RUNNING OUT OF MONEY
3. STOCK MARKET CRASH
4. PAY TOO MUCH IN TAXES
5. TIME WITH KIDS & GRANDKIDS
6. MORE TIME TO PAINT, HUNT AND FISH

Next, we need to consider how to build other income streams to make up for the shortfall. We must not forget the power of inflation. In twenty years, when Bob and Carol are eighty-seven, they'll need approximately $10,000 a month—and not because their tastes have gotten more expensive. It's because things like health-care, property taxes, insurance, and more will have increased the cost of baseline living.

HOW CAN YOU AVOID MISTAKES WITH CLAIMING SOCIAL SECURITY BENEFITS AND CREATING YOUR RELIABLE RETIREMENT INCOME PLAN?

The income bucket on the B.O.S.S. Retirement Blueprint™ gives you vision and clarity regarding where your income will come from on your retirement journey.

If you would like to see what your customized Social Security analysis and your retirement income would look like, you can visit www.GetMoreWithBOSS.com, and within minutes you will see how you could optimize your Social Security benefits now.

In addition, we can help you create a customized income plan that includes the right options for additional income streams, like dividends, annuities, bonds, and more—we did just that for Bob and Carol. The more tailored a plan, the higher the likelihood it will be effective.

WHAT'S NEXT?

So, we've made some good progress as it relates to retirement. You now know how much cash you have and how much you need based on your initial blueprint planning. You're also ready to finalize an income plan that starts with Social Security, and you know that you need at least three reliable retirement income streams in the income bucket. Do you want to grow your savings to keep up with inflation? That starts with understanding how to appropriately manage risk.

7

The Risk
Solution

While we were in college, we ran a business in the summers staining and sealing million-dollar cabins in Heber and Park City, areas in Utah. That's the job we mentioned in Chapter Six—the one where we made as much between May and September as some college graduates made all year. We learned a lot with that venture, but one lesson in particular sticks out when we consider risk.

Some cabins were tall enough that we used a forty-foot ladder. Some of the cabins we worked on were three stories, and they weren't always finished—meaning we had to get creative. At times, the big ladder could be balancing on rocky ground or unstable dirt, teetering from side to side. One of us was at the top, and the other was holding the bottom for more stability. Whoever was at the top was handling the sprayer, trying to reach into the eves and the top of the cabin while not losing their balance.

Inevitably, as we sprayed the top of cabins, we'd spray the ladder too. The person on top of the ladder—already on shaky ground—then had to climb down it, slippery aluminum and all.

As you can already envision, heights, metal, an oil-based product, and rubber tennis shoes don't mix.

In one unfortunate incident, one of our team members had an accident for that exact reason. He was up high, spraying near an aluminum roof. We looked up and saw him step onto the roof and slide—faster and faster, like the sled in the movie *Christmas Vacation*! The next thing we knew, he was sliding down the roof and then off the roof, down two stories quicker than we could blink.

Luckily, he was unharmed, and we learned a valuable lesson about minimizing risk!

HOW INVESTMENT RISK COULD COST YOU A SMALL FORTUNE

The stock market can be a scary place. It can feel like you are up on the forty-foot ladder with an oil-based stain and rubber tennis shoes! The first step to protecting yourself and your retirement savings is to understand how much risk you are taking with your investments and deciding if you are comfortable with that much risk.

In working with thousands of families, we rarely have a family that is approaching retirement or living in retirement feel comfortable with risking 30%–50% of their life savings because of the potential for a stock market crash or correction. Yet, unfortunately, many potential clients continue risking that amount because they have not matched their investment strategy with their appropriate tolerance for risk.

SOLUTION: THE B.O.S.S. RETIREMENT RISK REPORT™

In our risk and fee analysis, we stress test your portfolio to make sure you're not taking on too much risk at the worst possible time. What do we mean by stress test? In an example from another industry, when the FDIC audits a bank, an auditor will come in and make sure the bank would not likely fail if there were to be a recession or other large downturn in the economy. In short, we use the same process with your investment and retirement accounts.

DON'T LOSE THIS MUCH MONEY!

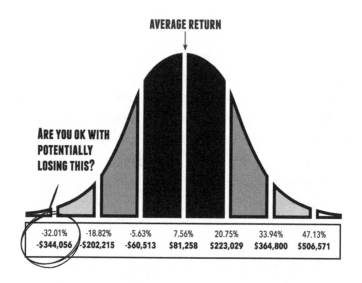

This is usually an enlightening experience for our potential clients. Likely for the first time in their lives, they have a window into whether their portfolios would lose money in the downturn of a market—or, even worse, lose even more with a major crash like the ones the market experienced in 2001 or 2008.

With this analysis, you have insight into what would happen to your investments if you suffered a major loss—not only as a percentage, but in dollars and cents.

It's important to note that nobody has a perfect crystal ball. Nobody knows when exactly the market will go down—but what comes up, must come down. That's why you need a strategy to understand your risk and make adjustments, if necessary, to protect your retirement savings.

HOW MUCH ARE YOU PAYING IN FEES?

Let's get real: if you are like most people, you have no clue what you're paying in fees for your retirement accounts. At B.O.S.S. Retirement Solutions and Advisors, we strive to make this as transparent as possible so that you know with clarity what you're paying.

The second goal of the B.O.S.S. Retirement Risk Report™ is to take a deep dive into the fees that you are currently paying in your accounts. When you come in and see us, you bring all your statements, and we're able bring clarity...perhaps for the first time for you... into those confusing documents and help you break down exactly what it is you are paying on each and every holding.

This includes those often-overlooked additional mutual fund costs. Then, we show you in real dollars, not a percentage, what you are paying in fees.

Let's take a look at Bob and Carol's investments and how we can measure their risk with our cutting-edge analysis that gives them a crystal-clear picture of their investments and the fees they are paying.

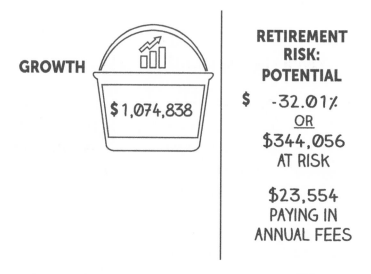

GROWTH — $1,074,838

RETIREMENT RISK: POTENTIAL

$ -32.01%
OR
$344,056
AT RISK

$23,554
PAYING IN
ANNUAL FEES

CASE STUDY: THE B.O.S.S. RETIREMENT RISK REPORT™ FOR BOB AND CAROL

In Bob and Carol's case, their B.O.S.S. Retirement Blueprint™ shows their growth bucket holds just over

$1 million in retirement savings in their 401(k) and IRA accounts.

It's been a hard road, though. In the Great Recession, they lost 40% of their portfolio. They're happy now that it's built back up, but the last thing they want to do is have that happen again—especially right before they are considering retirement.

When Bob and Carol came and met with us for the first time, they brought all their statements, including their 401(k) and IRA statements. We examined their stocks, bonds, and mutual funds, and we completed the risk and fee analysis for them.

Initially, they told us they would only be comfortable losing 10%. After the test, we found they were taking on far more risk than they had imagined. In fact, they discovered that they could lose more than 32% or **$344,056** in the next crash.

When Bob and Carol realized how much money they could lose in a market crash, they were not comfortable with taking on that much risk. They determined to make some adjustments to their investment strategies which reduced their risk to a level they were more comfortable with, especially as they were nearing retirement.

Bob and Carol's goal was to reduce their risk so no more than $100,000 or approximately 10% of their portfolio was subject to potential losses in the stock market. This move could help them keep an additional **$244,056*** in their pockets even if the market crashes—helping them have peace of mind with their hard-earned retirement savings.

[*Disclaimer—any investments in securities are subject to risk of loss. Past performance does not ensure future results.]

In the fee section of the B.O.S.S. Retirement Risk Report™, we helped Bob and Carol see they were losing a ton in fees: mutual fund fees, advisory fees, and more. They were shocked to find they were paying a combination in fees totaling 2.19% per year, adding up to $23,539 annually—all for the opportunity to potentially still lose money!

WHAT'S NEXT?

What will most likely be your largest expense during retirement? This one may surprise you…here is a hint…

It's not your mortgage…

It's not your healthcare…

It's not your long-term care…

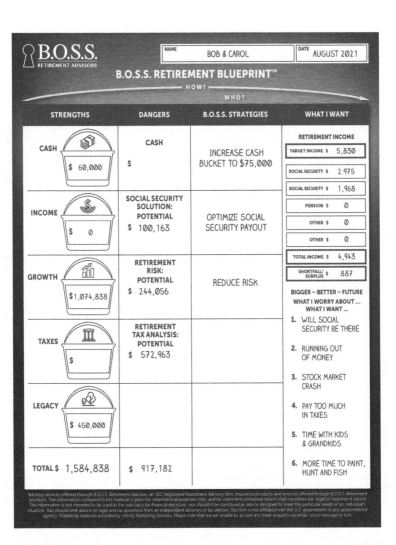

B.O.S.S. RETIREMENT ADVISORS

NAME	DATE
BOB & CAROL	AUGUST 2021

B.O.S.S. RETIREMENT BLUEPRINT™

HOW?

WHO?

STRENGTHS	DANGERS	B.O.S.S. STRATEGIES	WHAT I WANT
CASH $ 60,000	CASH $	INCREASE CASH BUCKET TO $75,000	**RETIREMENT INCOME** TARGET INCOME $ 5,830 / SOCIAL SECURITY $ 2,975 / SOCIAL SECURITY $ 1,968
INCOME $ 0	SOCIAL SECURITY SOLUTION: POTENTIAL $ 100,163	OPTIMIZE SOCIAL SECURITY PAYOUT	PENSION $ 0 / OTHER $ 0 / OTHER $ 0
GROWTH $1,074,838	RETIREMENT RISK: POTENTIAL $ 244,056	REDUCE RISK	TOTAL INCOME $ 4,943 / SHORTFALL/SURPLUS $ 887
TAXES $	RETIREMENT TAX ANALYSIS: POTENTIAL $ 572,963		**BIGGER – BETTER – FUTURE** WHAT I WORRY ABOUT... WHAT I WANT... 1. WILL SOCIAL SECURITY BE THERE
LEGACY $ 450,000			2. RUNNING OUT OF MONEY 3. STOCK MARKET CRASH 4. PAY TOO MUCH IN TAXES 5. TIME WITH KIDS & GRANDKIDS
TOTAL $ 1,584,838	$ 917,182		6. MORE TIME TO PAINT, HUNT AND FISH

Here's the answer: **it will most likely be taxes.**

And with the recent massive amounts of stimulus for COVID-19 relief, underfunded Social Security and Medicare…it will likely get MUCH worse!

Let's have a serious look at the tax bucket of the B.O.S.S. Retirement Blueprint™!

8

The Tax Solution

In Chapter Three we discussed the avalanche of taxes that could crush your retirement. When you understand that you could be taxed on your Social Security benefits, your pension income, and your 401(k) and IRA, in addition to paying property tax, sales tax, and gas tax at the pump, you start to realize the magnitude of the avalanche.

The bottom line...taxes could be, for you, the largest expense in retirement, but the good news is that in most cases, you can do something about it!

Taxes are one of the areas that you could really move the needle by saving tens of thousands, if not hundreds of thousands, of dollars in taxes!

How Big Is Your Retirement Tax Problem?

The key to minimizing the taxes you will pay in retirement is first to measure the size of your potential tax problem. When it comes to tax planning…ignorance is not bliss! After you measure the size of the potential tax problem you are facing in retirement, you can work with our recommended team of professionals to help you create a strategy to minimize your tax.

At B.O.S.S. Retirement Solutions and Advisors, we have a technology to help you look forward into retirement and measure the potential taxes you will pay, including taxes on required minimum distributions (RMDs), investment gains, and the taxes due on your 401(k) and IRA when you pass away. This technology is what we call the B.O.S.S. Retirement Tax Analysis™.

YOUR B.O.S.S. RETIREMENT TAX ANALYSIS™

The B.O.S.S. Retirement Tax Analysis™ is a customized report that offers insight into not only what you'll be paying in taxes this year, but also five years from now, ten years from now, twenty years from now, and throughout your retirement.

The report is simple, direct, and helps you to see clearly the avalanche of taxes waiting to crush your retirement dreams if you don't take action.

In addition, your eyes will be opened to gain insight on the following:

- How required minimum distributions (RMDs) are calculated.

- The annual remaining balances in IRAs after RMDs are withdrawn.

- How much of the RMD the client could hold on to after paying taxes.

- The potential cash available to reinvest from after-tax RMDs, per our recommendations.

- The potential cash available if after-tax RMDs are spent.

To help you envision what this looks like, let's take a fresh look at Bob and Carol's retirement tax analysis.

CASE STUDY: THE B.O.S.S. RETIREMENT TAX ANALYSIS™ FOR BOB AND CAROL

In Bob and Carol's case, their B.O.S.S. Retirement Blueprint™ shows the potential taxes they will face in retirement. In fact, paying too much in taxes is their number-one concern.

When we ran Bob and Carol's retirement tax analysis, we knew they'd saved just over $1 million. Their problem? Recall that in the alphabet soup—the 401(k)s, IRAs, TSPs, 403(b)s, and so forth—the number you see is not all your money.

In Bob and Carol's case, we discovered they could have to pay $884,666* in taxes on their $1 million 401(k) from age seventy-two (when they have to start taking out required minimum distributions) until age ninety, their life expectancy.

[*For illustrative purposes only. Actual results may vary.]

$884,666*
IN TAXES OWED!

[*For illustrative purposes only. Actual results may vary.]

CURRENT PRE-TAX QUALIFIED ACCOUNT
$1,074,838

KEEP QUALIFIED ACCOUNT		TAXES RARELY	
Total taxes paid on RMDs at time of withdrawals	$423,703	Taxes paid on conversion	$311,703
Taxes paid on reinvested RMDs	$172,544	Taxes paid on account growth	$0
Taxes paid on remaining account value at death	$288,419	Taxes paid on remaining account value at death	$0
Total Taxes Paid	$884,666	Total Taxes Paid	$311,703

DIFFERENCE OF $572,963

The above information is presented as a hypothetical scenario and is not intended as tax advice. The results shown are not guaranteed and will vary based on individual factors.

That is not a typo. That could have been their actual tax bill.

We helped them to create a plan to convert their assets to fall into the Taxed Rarely bucket, where those funds are taxed once and then under current tax law never taxed again. This had to be done in a systematic way to avoid penalties. Keep in mind that it doesn't erase taxes altogether—far from it. In Bob and Carol's case, they still owed $311,703 in taxes.

However, when you look at the difference between the two strategies, Bob and Carol were able to keep an additional $572,963 in their own pockets. We call that a big win.

$884,666–$311,703 = *$572,963* in tax savings!

So, the question for you is this...what would you do with an extra *$572,963* in retirement?

Imagine if you used this money to pay off excess debt, travel more, or even build that cabin you always wanted to build at the lake or in the mountains? Whatever your dream is, we believe it could start with the B.O.S.S. Retirement Tax Analysis™!

Your tax planning for retirement could be the biggest game changer for your retirement! Instead of dreaming... we invite you to take action and visit www.GetMoreWith-BOSS.com to see your own customized numbers and what it could mean in real dollars put back in your pocket to live your dreams!

WHAT'S NEXT?

Hopefully, by now you have a greater understanding of the reasons why retirement is complicated, and you see that the B.O.S.S. Retirement Blueprint™ is here to help you simplify the process of retiring and maximizing your money. Over the course of the last three chapters, we have delved deeply into the B.O.S.S. Retirement Blueprint™'s income, growth, and tax buckets, respectively, and you've seen Bob and Carol potentially maximize their retirement by an additional $917,182.

Let's take a look at how this new retirement vision comes together:

B.O.S.S. Retirement Blueprint™ benefits:

1. B.O.S.S. Social Security Solution™ $100,163

2. B.O.S.S. Retirement Risk Report™ $244,056

3. B.O.S.S. Retirement Tax Analysis™   <u>$572,963</u>

GET MORE WITH B.O.S.S. $917,182*

*[*For illustrative purposes only. Actual results may vary.]*

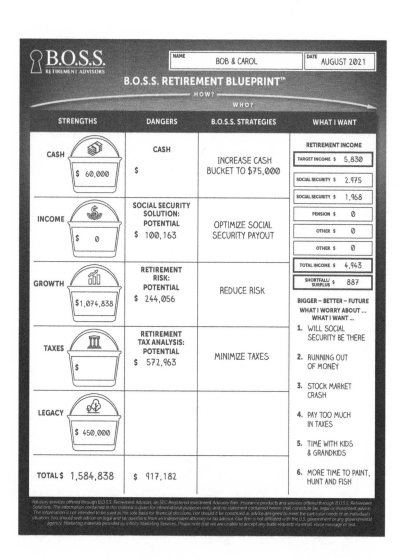

| | NAME | BOB & CAROL | DATE | AUGUST 2021 |

B.O.S.S. RETIREMENT ADVISORS

B.O.S.S. RETIREMENT BLUEPRINT™

HOW?

WHO?

STRENGTHS	DANGERS	B.O.S.S. STRATEGIES	WHAT I WANT
CASH $ 60,000	**CASH** $	INCREASE CASH BUCKET TO $75,000	**RETIREMENT INCOME**
INCOME $ 0	**SOCIAL SECURITY SOLUTION: POTENTIAL** $ 100,163	OPTIMIZE SOCIAL SECURITY PAYOUT	TARGET INCOME $ 5,830 / SOCIAL SECURITY $ 2,975 / SOCIAL SECURITY $ 1,968 / PENSION $ 0 / OTHER $ 0 / OTHER $ 0
GROWTH $1,074,838	**RETIREMENT RISK: POTENTIAL** $ 244,056	REDUCE RISK	TOTAL INCOME $ 4,943 / SHORTFALL/SURPLUS $ 887
TAXES $	**RETIREMENT TAX ANALYSIS: POTENTIAL** $ 572,963	MINIMIZE TAXES	**BIGGER – BETTER – FUTURE** **WHAT I WORRY ABOUT … WHAT I WANT …** 1. WILL SOCIAL SECURITY BE THERE 2. RUNNING OUT OF MONEY 3. STOCK MARKET CRASH
LEGACY $ 450,000			4. PAY TOO MUCH IN TAXES 5. TIME WITH KIDS & GRANDKIDS
TOTAL $ 1,584,838	$ 917,182		6. MORE TIME TO PAINT, HUNT AND FISH

Impressive, right? You bet it is. But there's something even more impressive: leaving a legacy for your family and those you care for.

Let's take the dollars and cents out. The most important question has nothing to do with money: what does all this mean to your life? To your peace of mind? To those you love?

What legacy do you envision leaving to those you love most or your favorite charity?

9

Leaving a Legacy

Our parents' legacy dream was to have a cabin in the mountains—a place where the family could gather and create memories. So, when we were growing up, Mom and Dad started that dream with a plan, and, starting in the late 1970s, they excavated the foundation and poured the foundation.

Slowly, working on it whenever they had the time and the cash...they added another chapter to their legacy. The dream of building the cabin had many starts and stops, like the Memorial Day mudslide of 1983, but nail by nail and board by board the cabin was built, and memories were created. Memories of the Fourth of July include barbeques, family reunions, and thousands of rocks thrown in the creek by grandkids.

Many years later, after Mom and Dad had retired, they lived in Cochabamba, Bolivia, for eighteen months on a mission with our church. As a result of an early October snowstorm, a pipe froze and flooded the cabin. Twenty-one thousand gallons of water from a second-floor bathroom destroyed the kitchen below, creating another messy chapter in Thacker cabin history.

Because they were away on their mission, we stepped in to help clean up the mess left behind by the flood. When we were discouraged about the flood, our mom sent us a beautiful and hopeful email giving us some insight and perspective about what legacy is really about. Here are some portions from this email:

> *One of our goals in building the cabin was to share Dad's great love of the mountains and also teach our family to work, love each other, and finish what we started. The great time we've had along the way has been a bonding experience that has also manifested in experiences each child has shared. What is a little water (OK, a lot of water), sheetrock, flooring, and cabinets compared to the work and fun we've had along the way? It's the process that's important.*

Each year we had a goal. As each part was planned and finished, we enjoyed ourselves along the way as we worked around everything else in life that was going on. What about stripping the forms off of the foundation the night before Megan was born?

After three years, the roof was on, and we started on the inside. Again, as we had money, we bought materials and found creative ways to build the cabin. I'll never forget how delighted Dad was when he came home and said he had an offer of free, shredded money from the US Mint to use as insulation in the bottom half of the sheetrock along the walls to insulate the cabin. We all had fun thinking about how much money that was.

Remember Dad getting permission to use the barn wood from the music store in the Cottonwood Mall as they were remodeling? We put it on the walls of the first floor for that rustic look that is perfect for the cabin.

As time went on, some years we did more, and some we did less, depending on cash flow, weddings, missions, church callings, etc. But the cabin has always been there, waiting for a good barbeque, some homemade ice cream, and a good family time. As grandchildren come along, everyone has been loved and included, and the stream is always waiting to have a few rocks thrown in.

So now, what do we do? The same thing that has always been done—we have a goal and a plan and keep working.

–LOVE, MOM

That's what legacy is all about—in our family, that is. In yours, legacy may look a lot different, and that's the beauty of the legacy bucket. It's yours to fill however you feel called and with whatever you're the most passionate about. It is your dream to dream, and your legacy to create.

When we think about legacy, we often think back to that critical moment when we lost it all financially. What saved us? Relationships. Our relationships with God, our families, our extended family, our work associates, and more. We think of our wives who stood by us and believed in us. The Latin phrase *summum bonum* expresses nicely how we feel: when you boil all these things down in life, the things that matter most are relationships. Then, the mental, physical, and financial assets become the icing on the cake.

It's not just the big moments, though, that define us. It's the relationships themselves—and the memories and closeness you take from them. We knew it before, but the downturn taught us to never, ever take that for granted. The whole way through, we relied on God to give us answers and to lead us and guide us every step of the way so that we could dig ourselves out of that hole. It was our faith in God and our strength in relationships that got us through.

Our mom essentially wrote the same idea in her email about the cabin. What ultimately matters are the relationships and the memories created with those we love most. The conversations that we have are the building blocks of those relationships.

We will create a plan from what you've been able to set aside for retirement, but that's not what matters most for somebody's ultimate legacy in retirement. There isn't a price on the memories you're able to make with each other, whether it's through serving in the community, spending time with your kids and grandkids, or exploring the world traveling.

It's important to note here, too, that building a legacy isn't a thing that just happens once. It's a process that occurs every day. It's in the little things. You don't need a cabin to flood or to lose $3 million to see it. (In fact, we hope neither of those things ever happens to you.)

For instance, take the example of the dad who gets up at six o'clock in the morning for forty years, just to make a paycheck for his family. Look at the mom who gets the kids off to school every. single. day. Look at the love that's built into those little actions—that are not little at all, really, but truly grand in their sacrifice.

You build your legacy day by day, making small deposits in your legacy bank the more time you spend with those you love and doing what you all love to do. The process of living your life on your terms and based on what matters most to you creates your legacy. The B.O.S.S. Retirement Blueprint™ gives you the vision to help you create the legacy you want...even after you pass away.

GETTING YOUR FINANCIAL HOUSE IN ORDER WITH YOUR ESTATE PLAN

Throw your greatest moments out the window, and instead think about the moments that made you better because they were hard. We've sat with thousands of families in our offices, and what they truly say when we discuss legacy is what they learned from all the challenges in their lives. They don't want to go back to those moments. So that is why it is so important to have a plan.

As you envision how you want to create a legacy, we're going to help you, as part of the B.O.S.S. Retirement Blueprint™, to get all the most important things in order as they relate to your finances. We assist with estate planning, wills and trusts, financial power of attorney, medical directives, and more. In a time of grief or confusion, you don't want any surprises. More than that, only *you* understand what's important to you when it comes to your legacy. We connect you with the right legal team to do the paperwork to help you make it known. Estate planning is not a do-it-yourself project…one mistake could cause you to lose a small fortune if it is not done correctly.

CASE STUDY: BOB AND CAROL'S LEGACY

Over the course of the last three chapters—while diving deeply into the B.O.S.S. Retirement Blueprint™'s income, growth, and tax buckets, respectively—you've seen Bob and Carol potentially maximize their retirement by $917,182. What has that meant to their lives?

When discussing the legacy bucket, we helped Bob and Carol unearth what legacy meant to them and worked to bring that to reality. We found they had a basic will, but the documents needed updating. After they were finalized, they could happily get on a plane and not have that nagging feeling that they weren't prepared in case of an emergency.

You'd be surprised how many couples don't do this. We've seen families—those who haven't worked with us—who have shoeboxes full of disheveled papers. Deciphering what's what is like putting a mystery together. Why? Nobody ever talked about their finances and where everything was. Luckily, this was easy for Bob and Carol to commit to, for more reasons than one.

In the end, not only could they sleep when the wind was blowing, but they could wake up refreshed and ready to make new memories—fishing, painting, and doing what they loved with the people they loved. Little legacy deposits, every day.

Now, it's your turn to take action and put the powerful principles you have learned in this book to work so you can enjoy a secure and independent retirement optimized with the B.O.S.S. Retirement Blueprint™!

10

Bringing It All Together

As Robert Frost famously wrote, "Two roads diverged in a wood, and I—I took the one less traveled by, and that has made all the difference."

You're there too. You're at that fork. We know your situation is different from Bob and Carol's. We know it's different from that of your neighbor. How are we so sure? We've helped thousands of families just like yours, and no two circumstances are ever exactly alike.

The patchwork of financial decisions that have gotten to you to this point have not been cookie-cutter. Likewise, your retirement dreams are not cookie-cutter. And your plan for retirement should not be cookie-cutter either.

As we helped Bob and Carol, we want to help you get to and through retirement with clarity and confidence. We started this book as your guide to help you see clearly the obstacles you will face in retirement.

Now it's your turn to overcome these obstacles with the strategies of the B.O.S.S. Retirement Blueprint™!

You could choose to stay on the path you're on, knowing that if you stay on this path, it could mean unreliable income in retirement, taking on more risk, potential losses with your investments, and needlessly paying tens of thousands, if not hundreds of thousands, of dollars or more in needless taxes...

Or you could choose the B.O.S.S. Retirement Blueprint™...a path that leads to peace of mind and confidence by having a plan which could give you the freedom to do what you've always dreamed of in retirement.

If you say "yes," you'll put to work for you some of the most talented and incredible people, as well as some incredible forces, that are going to lead you down this road, helping you discover the strategies of a proven system based on your goals for a secure and independent retirement.

Imagine the freedom you could feel if you had an income plan that includes your Social Security, an investment plan to protect your hard-earned retirement savings from losses, and a plan to minimize taxes.

On the other hand, if you say "no" and continue on the path of traditional investing and financial services, you're at the mercy of those who create and sell financial products with no plan. When we have another major stock market crash like we had in 2008 or 2001, where will that leave you?

Is that a risk you're willing to take with your retirement future?

Let's take a look at Bob and Carol one last time.

By having their B.O.S.S. Retirement Blueprint™, they could now have:

$100,163 more in lifetime Social Security benefits.

$244,056 protected from risk of loss.

$572,963 of tax savings with their retirement accounts.

$917,182 total.

THE B.O.S.S.
RETIREMENT
BLUEPRINT

VISION

THE B.O.S.S.
SOCIAL SECURITY
SOLUTION

$100,163

THE B.O.S.S.
RETIREMENT
RISK REPORT

$244,056

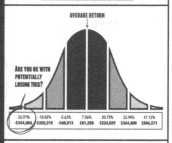

THE B.O.S.S.
RETIREMENT TAX
ANALYSIS

$572,963

TOTAL: $917,182

Of course, your situation is different, and your results will vary based on your individual circumstances. However, the goal is to help you optimize your hard-earned retirement savings with the B.O.S.S. Retirement Blueprint™.

WHAT IS YOUR GET MORE WITH B.O.S.S. NUMBER?

Visit www.GetMoreWithBOSS.com to see your "Get More" number. In just a few minutes, after entering some basic information, you'll receive a customized Get More with B.O.S.S. Number that will show you the potential amount your retirement could be optimized. This will give you vision and clarity regarding what is possible and how to make your retirement dollars go further in retirement.

Build your customized B.O.S.S. Retirement Blueprint™. Meet with a B.O.S.S. Retirement Advisor who can help you customize your blueprint to your specific needs and help you reach your retirement goals and build your legacy!

Give yourself the gift of freedom to start living the retirement you envision. You may be able to retire sooner than you think! Your B.O.S.S. Retirement Advisor can help you take the next step to fund your blueprint. This is the step that could help you enjoy a secure and independent retirement.

WHAT'S NEXT?

We have learned by helping thousands of families retire that money stress is one of life's biggest challenges. When you have too much stress over money, it affects everything in your life: your work, your family, and all of your relationships.

While no amount of money can buy true happiness, not having enough money to meet our needs both in life and retirement could certainly lead to unhappiness. Trust us on this one, because we've been there and know the feeling firsthand.

A better life won't just happen on its own. A better life happens when you take action to create it. As we've described in this book, the B.O.S.S. Retirement Blueprint™ is a powerful and proprietary process for producing incredible retirement results.

Remember, retiring successfully doesn't happen by accident…it starts with a plan, and that plan is the B.O.S.S. Retirement Blueprint™!

Whichever path you chose, we wish you all the best in your retirement future! We hope to make your retirement a reality soon!

Acknowledgments

Words cannot express our gratitude to all the friends and mentors who believed in our vision and helped in the creation of the B.O.S.S. Retirement Blueprint™.

We are grateful to the thousands of families who have chosen us to help guide them to and through retirement at B.O.S.S. Retirement Solutions and Advisors. You are the reason we exist! Thank you!

To our dedicated team, helping the families we serve would be impossible without your tireless dedication and passion for the mission of helping families retire with confidence. You embody all that is good and right with the world! We love you!

This book would have never been possible without the input over the years of our friends, colleagues, and all our valuable partners. Special thanks to Joe Bayliss and all our friends at Advisors Excel, especially David Callanan, Cody Foster, and Jason Lueger.

To our parents, who raised us to always be of service to others and to help make the world a better place than we found it—thank you for giving us the vision of what creating a legacy is all about and providing an amazing childhood that prepared us for life.

To our children, we hope that the lessons learned early in your life from the principles of the B.O.S.S. Retirement Blueprint™ will provide you the foundation to dream big and always make your future bigger than your past!

Finally, yet most important, to our wives—thank you for your love and for all of the support and encouragement you have given. Thank you for sharing our vision and for allowing us to pursue our dreams. We love you!

About the Authors

Tyson and Ryan Thacker are owners and cofounders of B.O.S.S. Retirement Solutions and Advisors. Over the course of their decades in the industry, about which they are passionate, the two brothers have helped thousands of families plan their way to and through secure retirements. Not only are they the authors of this book and other publications, they also host a weekly radio and television show to spread their message of careful and legacy-based retirement planning. In 2018, they were nominated as Ernst & Young Entrepreneurs of the Year, and their business has been named to Inc. 5000's Fastest Growing Companies List the past five years (and counting). Their firm has also been named Utah's Best of State for Retirement Planning and Investment Advisory Services two years running.